BIG PAPI

THE LEGEND AND LEGACY OF DAVID ORTIZ

CONTENTS

David Ortiz's two-run homer on April 12, 2016, produces a standing ovation.

The Boston Globe

Copyright © 2016 and 2022 by The Boston Globe

This book is available in quantity at special discounts for your group or organization. For further information, contact:

Triumph Books LLC
814 North Franklin Street
Chicago, Illinois 60610
www.triumphbooks.com
@TriumphBooks

TRIUMPH
B O O K S

TRIUMPHBOOKS.COM
@TriumphBooks

Printed in U.S.A.
ISBN: 978-1-63727-180-3
This is an unofficial publication. This book is in no way affiliated with, licensed by, or endorsed by MLB, David Ortiz, or the Boston Red Sox.

▶ **BOOK STAFF**
EDITOR Janice Page
ASSISTANT EDITOR Ron Driscoll

WRITER John Powers
ART DIRECTOR/DESIGNER Ryan Huddle

RESEARCHERS/PROOFREADERS
Paul Colton, Richard Kassirer, Ted Kehoe, James Matte, Joe Moore, James Page

FOREWORD

BY PEDRO MARTINEZ

I call David my compadre, my godbrother.

We shared the same agent [Fernando Cuza] when he was coming up in the minor-league system. We both grew up southwest of Santo Domingo, and I was always looking out for him because he was younger.

David is a unique kind of person and player, and he's never changed. One day, I dropped by a restaurant in Santo Domingo and I saw him receiving a phone call. I thought I was going to get the same David I was accustomed to seeing, with a huge smile, but instead he was a little bit sad and disturbed.

I asked him, "Why are you so down?" When he told me the Minnesota Twins had released him, I said, "Great." He said, "My daughter was born two weeks ago and I just got released. How can that be great?"

It was one of the few times I ever saw David serious toward me. I told him it was great because now I can get you to the Red Sox. From that moment, I kept trying to reach Theo Epstein, until I finally got ahold of him at 2:30 in the morning. I couldn't be prouder of having the opportunity to influence the Red Sox to bring him in.

David's attitude, the way he's performed in the big games, anything I can say will fall short. What David has done is unbelievable. Since he got to Boston, David was destined to have those opportunities, to carry the entire team to a championship.

It's the same with his attitude in the clubhouse. He learned a lot from me: Always treat everybody with class and respect. I went out there really determined to win and to try to do things right. David learned from that, he learned a lot from Manny Ramirez about hitting, and he's very grateful to have learned so much from all of us.

Even though we didn't pull it off in 2003, everything was in place for us to come back in 2004. The entire team had a never-give-up attitude and a lot of it had to do with David – he was always positive, always fighting.

I look at 2013, and people say that team overachieved.

I don't see it that way – I would say they did what they set out to achieve. Boston is electric; it's a place that can influence anybody coming in to play. The beards that those guys grew reflected the harmony they had in the clubhouse. The bombing in Boston unified the entire nation along with David and the players to go out and achieve that 2013 World Series. Everything was destined to happen and David was at the center of it.

They say it's hard to play in Boston, but it all comes with the attitude. David and I are very similar – we're very outgoing, we're very happy campers, but we compete with the best of them and we are very serious about it when it matters. The things David was able to do identified him with Boston. It's a very good marriage between David and the fan base and the passion they have about their team.

I am extremely fortunate to have shared with David what looks to me like our destiny. We were destined to be together, to be in the right place at the right time, to share the same success. David and I were very fortunate to have come out of probably the roughest area that you can think of when it comes to poverty – both of us went through it, and I consider both of us blessed because we came out successful.

I can't wait to be sitting behind David five years from now, giving that [Hall of Fame] speech. David can also be very emotional – I can't wait to see how much joy he is going to show. To see him on the same team with me and the greats of the game, a team that no one will be able to separate us from – that's one I am looking forward to.

I will be a proud older brother.

Ortiz gives Pedro Martinez a hand as Martinez leaves a game in June 2003, and the pair embrace after completing their stunning 2004 ALCS comeback at Yankee Stadium.

Ortiz urges Red Sox fans to stay "Boston Strong" after the 2013 ALCS, and accepts his 2004 World Series ring from principal owner John Henry on Opening Day 2005.

INTRODUCTION

BY JOHN HENRY

When we took over stewardship of the Boston Red Sox in early 2002, many of the building blocks for success were in place: the game's most beloved ballpark, the most knowledgeable and by far the most passionate fans in baseball, a strong group of talented players, and a stirring rivalry with our closest geographical opponent.

But there were significant challenges. Our rival, the New York Yankees, had gone to the World Series four consecutive years, winning three times. The Sox hadn't won a World Series since 1918, and in 2001, won just 11 of their last 34 games.

Even so, we set out on what felt like a quixotic, epic quest to take on the Yankees and bring the World Series back to Boston – not once but repeatedly. That was our promise.

The Sox hadn't been on a level playing field with the Yanks since the 1940s. Change was needed, and right away. We pledged to revitalize Fenway Park and implemented a fresh organizational philosophy, one that involved making new, vital commitments to the community.

We won 93 games in our first season but failed to make the playoffs. We needed a difference-maker. We found a most improbable one in David Ortiz, who at the time was a 27-year-old slugger of modest credentials whose former team had dropped him, making him a free agent.

How David ended up signing with the Sox that winter before the 2003 season is remembered differently by those involved, which tends to happen when legends are recounted. What we do know for sure is that it was our ace, Pedro Martinez, who brought David to our attention, for which Red Sox fans will be forever grateful.

We now had a giant in our midst, one who lifted the Sox and an entire region onto his broad shoulders. David not only became one of the greatest clutch hitters in baseball history, he elevated the sport by the sheer force of his infectious personality. Who will ever forget the bear hugs, the omnipresent bling, the deep-throated laugh, the huge grin freely offered to teammates, fans – even opponents! That personality dominated every stage on which he appeared, whether it was on the field, in the community, on behalf of the David Ortiz Children's Fund or the Red Sox Foundation.

David not only played a transcendent role in the greatest comeback in sports history against the Yankees in 2004, with two walkoff hits in the span of one calendar day, but was the connective thread to the three World Series titles the Red Sox won in 2004, 2007, and 2013. His performance in the '13 Series, at age 37, ranks among the greatest ever, as he batted a majestic .688 (11 hits in 18 at-bats), reached base 19 times in six games, and was named World Series MVP. The Sox struck out 59 times in that series; David struck out once.

I remember a conversation we had at a party a couple months later, while sitting next to a Christmas tree.

"I don't understand why they kept throwing me fastballs," he said.

I answered, "Because no one could hit them. They were devastatingly good. But you did."

As none of us will ever forget, 2013 was a year of tragedy in Boston, its world-famous marathon senselessly attacked by terrorists, a tableau that sadly has been repeated in all too many cities around the globe. Our region and our baseball team coalesced into "Boston Strong" that year, David taking the microphone at Fenway Park and defiantly urging us all to resolve that we would not be cowed by terrorism.

Our entire season was infused with a purpose that went far beyond the winning of baseball games, which gave added poignancy to our celebration in October, the first time in 95 years that Fenway Park witnessed a Series clinching.

For me, for all of us, David's career has been nothing short of magical. There are so many stories like this one from his final season, when he promised a home run to an indomitable little boy named Maverick Schutte. Maverick was 6, David was 40, but they became fast friends after Kevin Millar, a mutual pal, introduced them. It was Millar who told David of how Maverick had undergone 30 surgeries after being born with a heart defect.

"Always stay positive," David told Maverick in a video that was sent to the child. "Keep the faith."

David pointed emphatically into the camera. "You take care, buddy," he said, "and I'm going to hit a homer for you tonight. Remember that. For you."

We know better than to expect our heroes to perform great feats on demand. But that night, David delivered, hitting the first pitch he saw in the eighth inning off Yankees reliever Dellin Betances for a tie-breaking, game-winning home run. Back home in Wyoming, Maverick watched and cheered.

"What I was trying to do," David told reporters afterward, "was make Maverick feel happy, and have that connection with him. You throw that out there, just to make sure he has a friend he can count on right here."

In 20 years in big-league baseball, the last 14 with the Red Sox, David made profound connections with all of us, connections that were personal, heartfelt, and meaningful. So fitting, truly, that we called him "Big Papi." Who knew that a baseball player could ever feel so much like family.

EARLY YEARS

BIG PAPI // THE LEGEND AND LEGACY OF DAVID ORTIZ////////////////////

DOMINICAN DRIVE AND A
MINNESOTA MISSTEP

BY JOHN POWERS

He originally wanted to be Michael Jordan.

David Ortiz was an imposing manchild who could make plenty of space for himself beneath a basketball rim. But if you lived in the Dominican Republic, your role models were Juan Marichal and Felipe Alou and the rest of the island's storied ballplayers. Once Ortiz vaulted the fence that separated the court from the diamond and swatted a home run in his first at-bat, he was hooked on horsehide.

Enrique Ortiz had been a promising pitcher but his burly son grew up swinging at bottle caps, doll heads, stuffed socks – anything that could pass for a baseball. By 16, David had been discovered by a local scout and passed on to the Florida Marlins, then an expansion franchise that was building a system from scratch.

"Dah-veed, you are going to play in the big leagues someday," his father assured him when he was cut loose, sore-elbowed, from the club's local prospects program after a few months. "Maybe it won't be with the Marlins, but that is their mistake. There are other teams to play for."

Ortiz ended up signing for $7,500 with the Seattle Mariners, who seasoned him for a couple of summers in the Arizona sun, then sent him to their affiliate

Ortiz, then a Twin, avoids a swipe tag by Red Sox second baseman Jeff Frye in a July 2000 game. Previous page: Fans watch a game at the "Lindos Suenos" or Beautiful Dreams field in El Mamon, Dominican Republic, not far from David Ortiz's birthplace of Santo Domingo.

in Wisconsin, where he was the Midwest League's best defensive first baseman (not a misprint) and hit .322 as the Timber Rattlers reached the 1996 championship round.

That made Ortiz an attractive trading piece and when the Mariners needed a third baseman for the stretch run, he suddenly found himself a Twin as the player to be named later in the Dave Hollins deal. "This was one of the best young hitters I've ever been around," observed Wisconsin manager Mike Goff, who said he "lost it" when he was told that Ortiz had been swapped.

Ortiz responded with a breakout year, zooming from A-ball to the majors in five months, hitting .317 with 31 homers and 124 runs batted in along the way. "He just stormed through our minor-league system," observed general manager Terry Ryan.

Minnesota, a losing club that needed offensive punch, plugged in Ortiz as its everyday first baseman in 1998. He was hitting .306 when he fractured the hamate bone in his right wrist, the slugger's occupational hazard, had surgery, and missed two months.

That was the beginning of an up-and-down ride in the Twin Cities that lasted for five years and was marked by injuries, confusion, and frustration. The mutual disenchantment between Ortiz and the club began

> "YOU ARE GOING TO PLAY IN THE BIG LEAGUES SOMEDAY. MAYBE IT WON'T BE WITH THE MARLINS, BUT THAT IS THEIR MISTAKE. THERE ARE OTHER TEAMS TO PLAY FOR."
>
> **– ENRIQUE ORTIZ,** AFTER SON DAVID HAD BEEN CUT BY THE FLORIDA MARLINS' AMATEUR FARM TEAM IN 1992 AT AGE 17

in spring training in 1999 when the Twins sent their 23-year-old strongman, who was hitting .137 with a dozen strikeouts in 51 at-bats, down to the Salt Lake Buzz for development.

After crushing Triple A pitching, Ortiz was back by September and in 2000 he was their main but miscast designated hitter, a basher for a club that wanted him to be a singles hitter. "Whenever I took a big swing, they'd say to me, 'Hey, hey, what are you doing?'" he recalled. "So I said, 'You want me to hit like a little (girl), then I will.'"

Ortiz never was quite sure what the club wanted from him and it didn't help that he and manager Tom Kel-

ly weren't on the same page. "I don't think he really liked me," Ortiz mused later. "I don't know why. That was his style, not just with me. He was hard on young players. He was the kind of manager who likes veteran players. He never liked me."

When Ortiz broke his right wrist sliding into home against the Royals (yet stayed in the game and hit a homer in his next at-bat) and missed nearly three months of the 2001 season, it was the beginning of his *annus horribilis*. His mother Angela was killed at 46 in an automobile accident on the first day of 2002. "She used to love just watching me hitting the ball," said Ortiz, who had her face tattooed on his right arm. "All she worried about was how I hit the ball."

Then, after having knee surgery in the spring to remove bone chips, Ortiz missed several weeks and went 43 games without a homer. His turnaround came after the All-Star break when he heated up with a 19-game hitting streak while the Twins ran away with the AL Central and made the playoffs for the first time in more than a decade, knocking off the Athletics in the divisional series.

"I felt like things were really starting to come together," Ortiz said in his 2007 autobiography "Big Papi: My Story of Big Dreams and Big Hits." "I had the best year of my career, a season I dedicated to my mother... I was starting to make good money playing in the big leagues and I was starting to build my confidence, and I was playing for a team that went to the American League Championship Series. I really thought that things were looking up."

But his days in Minnesota were finished. The club had a Gold Glove first baseman in Doug Mientkiewicz. Ortiz, who was making $950,000, was up for salary arbitration and the Twins, a small-market operation with a limited budget, didn't want to pay him what could have been twice as much. So they let him go in December in what Ryan later conceded was "a bad baseball decision."

"I thought I might get traded or something but I never thought about getting re-leased," said Ortiz. "It just didn't seem like the kind of thing that could happen. I was coming off a pretty good year and I was young and I thought there would be some team out there that would want to trade for a big dude like me."

Ortiz was a man with a point to prove in search of a wall to clear. The opportunity came in the Fens, where the Sox were revamping and, among other things, looking to replace Brian Daubach, whom they'd set free. Ortiz was four years younger, had similar stats, could split time at both first base and DH, and would play for less than half as much money. He also came highly recommended. Pedro Martinez called the Boston front office from Santo Domingo as soon as he heard that Ortiz was on the market and urged that he be signed; fellow countryman Manny Ramirez concurred.

After Ortiz pummeled the ball in the Dominican winter league and showed defensive deftness, club scouts urged general manager Theo Epstein to acquire him. There was little risk or expense and significant upside. "You're looking at a player with the potential to be a middle-of-the-lineup bat in the big leagues," reckoned Epstein, who inked Ortiz to a one-year deal for $1.25 million.

Ortiz became much more: the greatest clutch hitter in Sox history, who helped put three rings on his teammates' fingers; the supersized face of the franchise; and a civic icon.

BY ANY OTHER NAME, ALWAYS ORTIZ

BY NICK CAFARDO

David Ortiz, known in 1996 as David Arias, was the top defensive first baseman in the Midwest League for the Seattle Mariners' farm team. And when Minnesota Twins general manager Terry Ryan acquired Ortiz from the Mariners for veteran third baseman Dave Hollins later that year, he felt he had stolen a top hitting prospect.

Ortiz proceeded to skyrocket through the Twins' minor league system in 1997, hitting .317 with 31 homers and 124 RBIs.

Five years later, after the 2002 season, Ryan released Ortiz. Ryan has beaten himself up ever since.

"We just made a bad baseball decision," Ryan said.

"I can't say David ever did one thing wrong. He was one of our best hitting prospects. We put him on our 40-man roster when he was in A ball. He just stormed through our minor league system; played at three levels in one year."

And what was Seattle GM Woody Woodward thinking?

David Arias (Ortiz was then using his mother's surname) hit .322 with 18 homers and 93 RBIs for Wisconsin of the Midwest League, while also earning defensive honors at first base.

"We had our people scout the league that year and David really stood out," recalled Ryan. "When Seattle needed a third baseman because of an injury, they came to us and we settled on David as the player to be named later."

Woodward seemed desperate when his third baseman, Russ Davis, was slowed by an injury. Hollins was a veteran having a good season for the Twins, and Woodward earmarked him as Seattle's choice. Ortiz was sent to Minnesota.

In Woodward's defense, he had four players — Alex Rodriguez (123 RBIs), Ken Griffey Jr. (140 RBIs), Jay Buhner (138 RBIs), and Edgar Martinez (103 RBIs) — having huge years. He had a first baseman — Paul Sorrento — with 93 RBIs, and Martinez was the greatest DH of his era. The Mariners scored 993 runs that season.

Ryan didn't have that abundance of offensive firepower.

A young Justin Morneau was behind Ortiz, but he was being converted from catcher to first base. Doug Mientkiewicz was an outstanding defensive player at first base, but the DH spot was open.

"DHs are pretty valuable, especially the ones who have done the things he has done," said Ryan. "You want a complete guy, but that wasn't a problem with us. There was plenty of room for a DH."

"Minnesota did a nice job identifying David as the player they wanted," Woodward said. "We needed a third baseman and Hollins came over and did a nice job for us. We had a lot of good hitters on the major league side, so it was hard to project David down the road on our club, but when he got to Boston . . . he's had a great career."

Ortiz was 19 when he played for Mike Goff for Wisconsin in the Midwest League.

"He was tough, but I really liked him and he taught me a lot," Ortiz said. "He'd fine me all the time. Twenty-five or $50 for things. I didn't have any money. But at the end of the year, he gave it all back to me."

Goff wouldn't say what the fines were for.

"If I'd reveal that, David would probably shoot me," Goff said. "He was a wonderful kid. I loved him. He had a great year for me. At the start of the season, I didn't have a first baseman or a lefthanded hitter. People in the organization said he was having throwing problems. I just said the kid had a good year in rookie league and I need a lefthanded hitter and first baseman. They said, 'OK, but he'll be a 24th or 25th guy on the team.'"

Ortiz nearly won the Triple Crown.

Wisconsin got into the playoffs that year and lost in the league championship.

"It was right after the [final] game, and my phone rang. It was one of our farm people and I said, 'Please don't tell me David is the player to be named in the Hollins deal.'"

But that's what they told Goff.

"I lost it," Goff said. "This was one of the best young hitters I'd

ever been around. This kid was special. Imagine if we had David and Edgar Martinez on the same team?"

In fact, when he gave Ortiz his cash back, Ortiz said Goff told him, "You know why I was so hard on you? Because of all the players on this team, you're going to be the big leaguer."

"I'll never forget that," Ortiz said.

Ortiz said back then, the Seattle organization didn't pay much attention to players who weren't high draft picks. Latin players, he said, had a tougher time getting through the organization. Ortiz said it was a long haul for those players.

And when he was traded, "I was devastated," Ortiz said.

Ortiz loved Martinez, a player who spoke to Ortiz a lot in spring training, much like Ortiz does now to young Dominican players.

Conversely, Ortiz has no affection for then-Twins manager Tom Kelly, and Ortiz doesn't think there was any the other way, either. Ortiz loved John Russell and Al Newman, two managers who had him in the Twins' lower levels. And Ortiz never blamed Ryan for dumping him.

"Terry is a good man," Ortiz said. "Decisions are decisions. Just because you make a bad decision doesn't mean you're a bad person. I have a lot of respect for Terry. The decision he made wasn't all his."

On Kelly, Ortiz said, "I don't think he really liked me. I don't know why. He was hard on young players."

Ortiz said longtime Twins

manager Ron Gardenhire, who replaced Kelly in 2002, "was OK. I remember one time in 1998 after the season, I remember Gardy told me, 'See you next year if you're still here.'

"The following year they sent me down on the first cut. A lot of people do things they forget about, but we don't forget. If you don't want people saying things about you later, don't say it," Ortiz said.

Ortiz also remembers a bad moment in Seattle. He said he was going to receive a bat at the Kingdome for being the best hitter in the Mariners minor league system. Lou Piniella, the Mariners manager at the time, was supposed to present him with it.

"I was all excited ahead of time because I'm gonna shake the manager's hand. [Piniella] comes out on the field and basically threw the bat at me and walked away. That was very disappointing. I was like damn . . . OK. That's how it is? It was something I never forgot," Ortiz said.

In Minnesota, Ortiz was pla-

tooning at DH with Matt LeCroy. Ortiz finally broke out in 2002 when he hit 20 homers and knocked in 75 runs in 412 at-bats. He was going to get about $1.5 million in arbitration that year and the Twins decided to let him go. He settled with the Red Sox after they picked him up for $1.25 million.

Ryan disputes money was the factor.

"I hit 20 and knocked in 75 runs in 400 at-bats. Imagine if you give me 500-550 at-bats what that might lead to? I knew I was good. I knew I was a stud as a hitter, but I just couldn't prove it until I got the chance to play every day in Boston. And I had to wait for that because we had Jeremy Giambi," Ortiz said.

Theo Epstein had to be talked into picking up Ortiz by Red Sox international scout Louis Eljaua. Epstein balked because he had Giambi, but he still signed Ortiz. It was one of the best moves Epstein ever made.

"It's never been easy but that's good," Ortiz said. "That forces you to give everything you have. It's different when you have to fight your way through it. You don't take things for granted."

And as for his name, Arias or Ortiz?

"I haven't changed my name," Ortiz said. "When I was in Seattle they used to call me my mother's last name and sent my visa in my mother's name. When I got to Minnesota I straightened all that out. They said if something happens in the future we should call you by your father's last name. People think I changed my name, but I always went by Ortiz."

GLORY DAYS

BIG PAPI // THE LEGEND AND LEGACY OF DAVID ORTIZ

Ortiz hits a home run off the Yankees' Roger Clemens in July 2003, his first season with the Red Sox. Previous page: As the confetti flies, Ortiz salutes fans in Copley Square after the 2013 title.

BIRTH OF A LEGEND

BY JOHN POWERS

The first one was an autumnal preview of all the rest since. The Red Sox were down two games to one to the Athletics in the 2003 American League Divisional Series and were facing extinction at home, trailing 4-3 with two out in the eighth. Then David Ortiz, who'd been 0-for-16 with six strikeouts to that point in the series, launched a drive off future teammate Keith Foulke that bounced off the Oakland bullpen for the game-winning double, setting up his team to win the series on the road the next day.

"This is how guys are made heroes," observed first baseman Kevin Millar.

Thus did Ortiz make himself into Senor Octubre, the savior of seasons. All three of Boston's championship campaigns – 2004, 2007, and 2013 – bore Big Papi's timely thumbprints. None were more notable than the first of them, which ended 86 years of frustration and was made possible by Ortiz's consecutive wee-hour walkoffs that brought the Sox back from the dead against the Yankees in the American League Championship Series.

They were down three games to none after a brutal 19-8 home loss that concluded in a near-empty ballpark. "I thought about all the people I saw at the field that night, destroyed," said Ortiz, whose 10th-inning, two-out walkoff homer had clinched a divisional sweep of the Angels a week earlier. "I thought about us being in Boston. I

thought about how I don't like to lose. I'm not a loser."

So he won the next two games with two swings of the bat that turned the series around and produced the unlikeliest pennant in history. His 12th-inning blast off Paul Quantrill that landed in the New York bullpen at 1:22 a.m. set the stage for his game-winning, 14th-inning single the following night. "It was unbelievable," said outfielder Gabe Kapler. "It was Jordan-esque. It was remarkable, unparalleled, unrivaled."

After his confreres went on to close out the Yankees in the Bronx, Ortiz set the tone against the Cardinals in the World Series with a three-run shot in the first inning of the opener, the first home run by a Sox player in the Fall Classic at Fenway since Carlton Fisk's blast against the Reds in 1975. "Who's your Papi?" Sox fans asked the visitors.

Pitching to Papi when the leaves were falling was a risky notion. After Ortiz jacked a two-run homer into the right-field seats to bust apart the opener of the 2007 divisional series

against the Angels, manager Mike Scioscia walked him intentionally with two outs and the score tied in the ninth inning of Game 2, then watched Manny Ramirez hit a killer three-run homer. "It's hard to let David beat you," mused Boston manager Terry Francona.

When the Sox went on to a mile-high sweep of the Colorado Rockies that year, Ortiz delivered the first run-scoring punches in the final two games in Denver. And during the storied 2013 worst-to-first run, perhaps the most emotional of all of

> "YOU COULD SEE THAT ORTIZ WAS A GOOD HITTER IN MINNESOTA. BUT HE HAD HOLES. NOW THERE ARE NO HOLES, AND HE IS A LOT STRONGER."
>
> — **JOE TORRE**, YANKEES MANAGER, AFTER ORTIZ HAD PRODUCED WINNING HITS IN GAMES 4 AND 5 OF THE 2004 ALCS

Boston's championship seasons, he was simply thunderous. His two homers off ace David Price in the second game knocked Tampa Bay backwards in the divisional series.

And after the Sox were floundering against the Tigers in the league championship series, on the verge of losing the first two games at home, Ortiz turned things around with one swing in the eighth inning, a game-tying, two-out, line-drive grand slam into the Detroit bullpen that upended outfielder Torii Hunter, his legs facing skyward, matching a Boston cop's arms-up victory salute a few feet away. "Storybook. Like a movie," said third baseman Will Middlebrooks after the Sox had gone on to even the series, which they won in six games. "Down and away and he hits it 400 feet. That's just stupid, right? It does not make sense. But that's David for you."

The man whose defiant declaration in the wake of the Boston Marathon bombing had helped rally the city made sure that the year ended with a triumphant parade down the same street. The Cardinals could not get him off the Series stage as Ortiz batted .688, reached base 19 times in 24 plate appearances, and was named Most Valuable Player. "What planet is that guy from?" wondered teammate David Ross.

Planet Papi is most visible after the fall equinox. His postseason numbers are otherworldly with a .295 average, 17 homers, and 60 runs batted in across 17 series. "I'm not a beginning guy," he once declared. "I'm an end-of-the-season guy."

From far left: A 2004 title ring; Big Papi wore a big belt for the 2013 parade, surveyed Boylston Street after the 2004 title, and played the field as needed when the Sox were in Philadelphia and other NL parks .

2003: Clockwise from top left: Teammates and coaches celebrate Ortiz's walkoff homer against the Orioles; Pedro Martinez and Ortiz do some scoreboard-watching; forced out in Game 5 of the ALCS; Ortiz's bat fails him in a June game; Johnny Damon gives Ortiz a hand in an August victory.

2004:
The ALCS provided highlight-reel moments, including an eighth-inning homer in Game 5 that produced a sign of the times, and a game-winning blast in Game 4.

2004 POSTSEASON: A KEEPER

There's no way to fully explain or comprehend what came over David Ortiz in October of 2004. It was as if he'd struck some Faustian bargain with the baseball gods. Ortiz became the Walkoff Wonder, better than Babe Ruth, Mickey Mantle, Willie Mays, or Reggie Jackson.

In Greater Boston, we always thought of Carl Yastrzemski as the ultimate warrior of baseball's final month. Yaz didn't get many play-off opportunities, but he put up big numbers when it counted in 1967 and '75. He even homered off the unhittable Ron Guidry in the one-game AL East playoff with the Yankees in 1978.

But the great Yaz never did what Ortiz did in 2004. No one ever did.

11
RBIs FOR ORTIZ
IN 2004 ALCS

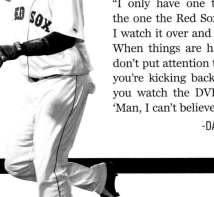

From Oct. 8-23, Ortiz enjoyed the greatest stretch of clutch hitting in postseason baseball history. He was Most Valuable Player of the AL Championship Series against the Yankees. He tied a record by knocking in 19 runs in the postseason – a record he reached in the first game of the World Series. He won three playoff games at Fenway with walkoff hits, within the span of 11 days. Two of his game-winners actually came on the same calendar day (Oct. 18).

Asked if he had a favorite moment, Big Papi smiled and said, "I only have one tape at home, the one the Red Sox made for us. I watch it over and over and over. When things are happening, you don't put attention to it, but when you're kicking back at home and you watch the DVD, you realize, 'Man, I can't believe I did that.'"

-DAN SHAUGHNESSY

2004:
Ortiz heads for first base after depositing his game-winning single in the 14th inning of Game 5 of the ALCS, and measures his game-winning home run off the Yankees' Paul Quantrill in the 12th inning of Game 4.

GAME 5, 2004 ALCS:
THE MAN OF THE HOUR

Heroes? Got an hour? There was David Ortiz. There was David Ortiz. And there was David Ortiz. The big guy started his team on the way back from a 4-2 eighth-inning deficit when he redirected a Tom Gordon pitch into the Volvo sign atop the Monster Seats. That's a prodigious poke for a lefthanded batter, by the way. As for his game-winning at-bat in the 14th inning, it was downright Boggsian, and it testifies to the type of hitter Ortiz has become. For Esteban Loaiza was pitching not just well, but downright brilliantly, and Ortiz fouled off five tough pitches before his winning base hit.

"Best stuff he's had since he's been with us," said Yankee manager Joe Torre, and that's no hyperbole. Loaiza made tough pitch after tough pitch, right down to the one Ortiz plopped in front of Bernie Williams to bring home Johnny Damon (who had drawn a one-out walk and moved to second on a Manny Ramirez walk) with the winning run.

Torre had remarked before the game that, "You could see that Ortiz was a good hitter in Minnesota. But he had holes. Now there are no holes, and he is a lot stronger."

Only a sophisticated hitter could have had that at-bat, and only a very strong one could have muscled that particular pitch over the infield (think vintage Jim Rice).

-BOB RYAN

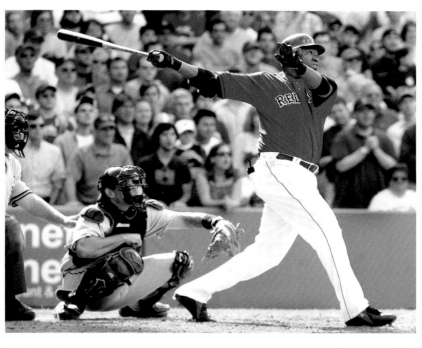

2005:
Clockwise from top left: A flying leap after his homer beat the Angels in September; a three-run homer tops the Orioles in June; Ortiz salutes his mother after a homer in the ALDS vs. Chicago; Ortiz rubs heads with Mike Timlin after a September win; sharing a spring-training cart ride with wheelman Kevin Millar, Manny Ramirez, and Jay Payton; Wally gets a tweak on the nose after a June win.

ORTIZ LED THE AMERICAN LEAGUE IN EXTRA-BASE HITS FOUR TIMES: 2004 (91), 2005 (88), 2007 (88), AND 2016 (87). HE WAS SECOND IN 2006, WITH 85.

2006:

Clockwise from top left: Escorting Jordan Leandre, 5, to sing the national anthem in April; solo homer vs. the Rays in September; teammates prank Ortiz by initially ignoring him after his 52nd homer; a walkoff homer beats the Indians in July; a postgame steal of the base after a stolen base in July; pressing the flesh after an August homer.

2007:
Clockwise from near right: Signing autographs before the September regular-season finale; showing off the October hardware; dugout greetings after a solo homer in July; saluting Manny Ramirez after an ALCS homer; bat drop after an August grand slam against the Angels.

"PEOPLE ARE USED TO SEEING YOU COME THROUGH ON EVERY AT-BAT AND DOING SOME DAMAGE. IT CAN'T ALWAYS BE THAT WAY. THIS IS NOT A NINTENDO GAME. THOSE ARE REAL PITCHERS OUT THERE TRYING TO MAKE A LIVING."

— **DAVID ORTIZ,** DURING AN INJURY-PLAGUED 2007 SEASON

2007 WORLD SERIES: LEADER OF THE PACK

I t would be impossible to overstate how critical David Ortiz was to Boston's championship run in 2007. He had become one of the most feared hitters in the game, and his presence in the lineup was a major benefit to those around him, specifically cleanup hitter Manny Ramirez. In the clubhouse, Big Papi was a dynamic, soothing personality who proved to be a confidant and friend to all, particularly the Latin players.

The Red Sox players respect Ortiz for his skills, but also his willingness to speak from the heart on their behalf. There is no bull with Big Papi; the big man prefers to tell it straight.

On the eve of the American League Championship Series, Ortiz lamented the lack of power on the Red Sox, pining aloud for the kind of lumber featured in the New York Yankees' lineup. Never mind the Yankees were already home, eliminated by the Indians in the first round.

"It can't always be me and Manny," Ortiz said. "We need some help, bro. I thought we would have gotten some [last winter]."

General manager Theo Epstein said the Red Sox front office had grown accustomed to impassioned Ortiz critiques and learned to put them in proper perspective.

"Sometimes I wake up and wish he didn't say some of the things he says," Epstein conceded, "but it almost always comes from a place of spontaneity and emotion. It never comes from a bad place.

"David really cares about winning. I never want to limit his emotion in any way, because he speaks from his heart. His personality has been critical to the success of our team. He brings all corners of the clubhouse together."

-JACKIE MACMULLAN

2007:
Curt Schilling, Kevin Youkilis, and other mates greet Ortiz after a September walkoff homer against the Rays.

2008:
Clockwise from near right: Ortiz performs his home-run ritual in March in Tokyo; a homer in a rehab start at Pawtucket, after a wrist injury in July; hugging Johnny Pesky after Pesky's No. 6 is retired in September; exchanging caps with members of the Hanshin Tigers at the Tokyo Dome.

10
TIMES AN AMERICAN LEAGUE ALL-STAR

23
FEWEST HRs IN A SEASON WITH RED SOX (2008, 2012) (BOTH INJURY-PLAGUED YEARS)

"THE WAY THAT HE TALKS, THE WAY THAT HE WALKS INTO A ROOM, ALL EYES TURN TO HIM."

– JOHN FARRELL,
RED SOX MANAGER

2009:

Clockwise from near right: Greeting Dustin Pedroia at spring training; a first-base laugh with the Orioles' Ty Wiggington; preseason work in the cage; batting vs. Boston College in Fort Myers; signing for a couple of adoring fans.

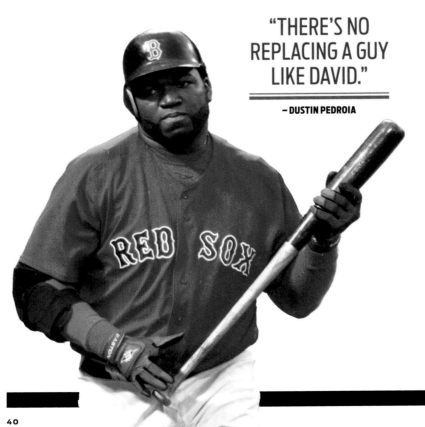

> ## "THERE'S NO REPLACING A GUY LIKE DAVID."
>
> **– DUSTIN PEDROIA**

2010:
Clockwise from far left: Doubling against the Yankees in May; roaming in enemy territory before the season opener with the Yankees; competing in the Home Run Derby in Anaheim before the All-Star Game (he won); tripling against the Jays in August.

2011:

A pat on the back for Dustin Pedroia in July; playing through the rain in May; circling the bases in Yankee Stadium after a homer off A.J. Burnett; view from the Green Monster seats for the home opener.

2012:
Clockwise from
far left: Snapping
his bat after
lining out against
the Orioles in
May; following
through on
a homer vs.
Seattle; working
out after an
Achilles-tendon
injury; walking
with son D'Angelo
at spring training;
escorting Johnny
Pesky and Bobby
Doerr with Jason
Varitek and Tim
Wakefield on
Fenway's 100th
anniversary;
seeking a fresh
start in February
with Kevin
Youkilis and
Adrian Gonzalez
after an ugly
end to 2011.

GAME 2, 2013 ALCS: AN EPIC GRAND SLAM

Close your eyes and it is 2004 all over again. Tom Brady is throwing last-second touchdown passes en route to a certain Super Bowl, David Ortiz is the greatest clutch hitter in baseball history, and the unwashed Red Sox are escaping from a hopeless deficit while Mayor Menino is pumping tires on the duck boats.

What might be the most exciting day in Boston sports history started with Brady's TD pass to beat the Saints with 5 seconds left and ended at festive Fenway at 11:44 p.m. when Jarrod Saltalamacchia singled to left, scoring Jonny Gomes from third to give the Red Sox an impossible 6-5, series-squaring, come-from-behind victory over the stunned Detroit Tigers.

In the day of all days, the moment of all moments was the Ruthian sight of Ortiz crushing a first-pitch, game-tying grand slam off Tigers closer Joaquin Benoit in the eighth inning. As right fielder Torii Hunter flipped spectacularly over the bullpen wall in fruitless pursuit of the flying seed, a Boston bullpen cop signaled "touchdown" and Fenway came to life.

This was not a walkoff. This was a liftoff. Flat on the ground for almost 17 strikeout-filled innings over two games, Boston's championship hopes were launched into the airspace over the Back Bay as 38,029 fans rattled Fenway's 101-year-old timbers.

"As we've seen, we're going to play to the final out," said Sox manager John Farrell. "David has come up big so many times in the postseason, none bigger than tonight.

Just an incredible comeback here."

"We needed it, man," said Ortiz. "I tried not to do too much. I wasn't trying to hit a grand slam. Just try to put a good swing on the ball. . . . I grew up playing with Torii. He's one of the best outfielders I've seen in my life. I think the ball took a left turn while he was turning right."

It was a Fisk-like moment.

Incredible? Unbelievable? Cosmic? Epic? Go ahead. Choose your word. This was right up there with any of the thrills we've seen at the ancient yard over the last century. Dave Roberts was summoned for the ceremonial first pitch and the event unfolded in a fashion reminiscent of the comeback against the Yankees in 2004.

In Foxborough or at Fenway, this was not a day to leave early.

All hope seemed lost at Yawkey Way. The Sox were striking out at a record pace – 17 times in a 1-0 defeat on Saturday and 13 more times in Game 2 as they fell behind, 5-1, through seven innings.

We were set to bury them. The Sox managed only one hit over the first 14 innings of the series. They were about to go down two games to none and face Justin Verlander in Game 3 in Detroit. After not losing four straight games all season, the Sox looked like candidates for a sweep in the ALCS.

It was 5-1 in the eighth when Tigers manager Jim Leyland got a little too cute and started a Joe Maddonesque parade of relievers. He wound up with big, nasty Benoit facing Ortiz with the bases loaded and two outs. Ortiz had already fanned twice on the night.

Papi struck on the first pitch. There was little doubt as his heat-seeking missile screeched toward the Sox bullpen. Hunter hit the wall at full speed and flipped as the ball soared beyond his reach. It was 5-5. It was already over.

"It's playoff baseball," said Leyland. "It looked like we had one in hand. We let one get away, no question about that, but these were two great games."

It cannot get better than this.

-DAN SHAUGHNESSY

2013:
The Tigers' Torii Hunter goes tumbling and Fenway erupts with Ortiz's grand slam in Game 2 of the ALCS; Ortiz homers off the Cardinals' Michael Wacha in Game 2 of the World Series.

2013:
Clockwise from far left: Ortiz is greeted after sliding home on a Mike Napoli double in World Series Game 1; helping with the champagne toast after celebrating the world title on the field; fans exult after the Game 2 ALCS slam vs. Detroit; joining Mayor Menino after a ceremonial ALDS first pitch.

.688

BATTING AVERAGE (11 FOR 16) IN 2013 WORLD SERIES

GAME 4, 2013 WORLD SERIES: TALKING THE TALK

David Ortiz, chairman of the impromptu gathering, didn't clear it with his manager. In fact, he didn't even consider such a thing. Protocol? What do you mean, protocol?

After all, it was the middle of Game 4 of the World Series, and the chance of another Red Sox title was slipping away faster than any radar gun could clock it. All Ortiz knew was that it was his time to talk.

"David doesn't script much," said Sox manager John Farrell, who watched with a blend of delight and admiration as Ortiz rallied the troops at Busch Stadium in St. Louis. "And that certainly wasn't scripted."

After the Sox went on to win their third world title in 10 seasons, Ortiz's dugout speech, his

Fall Classic carpe diem, pretty much stood as the Series' seminal moment.

Having fallen behind two games to one, the Sox were at the precipice of dropping two back in the best-of-seven series, their bats again turned meek by stout Cardinals pitching.

Enough of that, said Ortiz. The sole holdover from Boston's curse-busting team in 2004, he summoned his teammates, some of whom looked frustrated and forlorn, to one end of the dugout. It was time for them to wake up, shake the clouds of doubt, and sense the opportunity.

This was the World Series, the big man reminded them, and though not everyone wins when they get to October, there are scores of players, some among the game's greats, who never even get

the chance to attempt victory.

"Like I told my teammates, 'If you think you are [always] going to come to the World Series, you're wrong, especially playing in the AL East,'" he said later, his poignant words having helped the Sox rally to a 4-2 win that would ultimately lead to two more victories and a six-game conquest of the Cards. "Do you know how many people we beat to get to this level? To this stage? A lot of good teams, a lot of good teams, man, and that doesn't happen every year.

"I told them, 'It took me [six] years to get back up to this stage, and we had better teams than what we have right now and we never made it. So take advantage of being here.'"

Such was the crux of the Ortiz message. Sense the moment, seize it, before the dream of slipping on a diamond ring turns into a lasting choker of regret.

"I just saw a lot of faces, you know, looking in the wrong direction," he said. "And every team has that guy [to speak up] and I think I am that guy here."

Thus, in that instant, he became not David Ortiz the designated hitter but Big Papi, prophet of horse-hide-and-pine-tar resurrection. He talked. They listened. And they got it going, ignited by Ortiz's leadoff double in the fifth inning that was only the second hit off St. Louis starter Lance Lynn.

"His words were spot-on," said Farrell, who soon saw Ortiz wheel home with the run that tied the game, 1-1, on a Stephen Drew sacrifice fly. "I can't say everything that he said, but the message was spot-

.455
CAREER WORLD SERIES BATTING AVERAGE, BEST BY ANY PLAYER WITH AT LEAST 50 PLATE APPEARANCES

.576
CAREER WORLD SERIES ON-BASE PERCENTAGE, IN 59 PLATE APPEARANCES

2004, 2007, 2013
WORLD SERIES STATS

"THERE IS ALWAYS THIS CALMNESS ABOUT HIM. AND WHEN PITCHERS SEE THAT CALMNESS, I THINK IT WORRIES THEM."

– GABE KAPLER, SOX TEAMMATE FOR FOUR SEASONS

on. It was along the lines of, 'We've gotten to this point because of the players we are.' And I think what he was reflecting on is what we all sensed and felt, in that we weren't having normal or typical at-bats.

"It just felt like there was maybe an overarching mood that needed to be jolted and snapped out of, and that's what took place."

Ortiz ended the Series with a .688 batting average, but neither baseball-reference.com nor the Elias Sports Bureau keeps track of verbal grand slams such as the one Ortiz delivered in Game 4. In the inning after Ortiz's double helped bring the Sox even, Jonny Gomes submitted the kill shot, smacking a three-run homer over the wall in left for a 4-1 lead. The invisible tail on that comet had Ortiz's wisdom written all over it.

"Any time this guy steps in the box," said Gomes, "there's a presence. Any time this guy puts a uniform on, there's a presence. If this guy wants to rally us together for a pep talk, it was like 24 kindergartners looking up at their teacher. That message was pretty powerful."

All in all, said Gomes, the speech was the "little kick in the butt that we needed."

Infielder Xander Bogaerts just turned 21, the youngest of the Red Sox with a locker next to Big Papi. When Ortiz spoke, he was all ears.

"Whenever he talks, everyone listens. He's respectful to all of us and we give him the same respect. It was a pretty amazing moment."

It stands now as a moment that will last forever.

-KEVIN PAUL DUPONT

2014:
Clockwise from near right, Obliging fans on arriving at spring training; stringing together title and MVP rings on Opening Day; gesturing toward the press box after a ball he hit was ruled an error in June; eyeing an opposite-field homer vs. the Angels; tagged out at home trying to score against the Cubs in July.

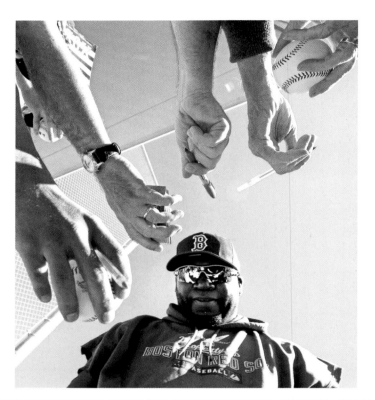

2015: Belting an opposite-field homer vs. the Marlins in July; being feted for his 500th homer, which came nine days earlier, on Sept. 12 at Tampa Bay; fans celebrate No. 502 vs. the Rays on Sept. 24.

"I'VE ALWAYS BEEN MY OWN HITTING COACH."

– DAVID ORTIZ

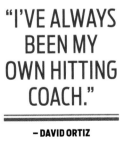

DAVID ORTIZ TOP 10 POSTSEASON MOMENTS

Ortiz doubles and goes on to score the first Boston run in pivotal Game 4 of the 2013 World Series.

2003 ALDS, GAME 4 VS. ATHLETICS

EIGHTH INNING, LOSING 4-3, VS. KEITH FOULKE
Two-run double to right field scores Garciaparra and Ramirez, wiping out one-run deficit and sending the series to Game 5, which the Sox win, 4-3, to set up ALCS vs. Yankees. Ortiz went just 2 for 21 in the ALDS, adding a single in Game 5.

2003 ALCS, GAME 7 VS. YANKEES

EIGHTH INNING, LEADING 4-2, VS. DAVID WELLS
Ortiz's long solo home run provides Boston with a 5-2 lead, with six outs to go and Pedro Martinez on the mound. What could possibly go wrong? After the Yankees rallied to tie it, Ortiz added a double in the top of the 10th inning, before Aaron Boone's home run provided the crushing final blow in the 11th.

2004 ALDS, GAME 3 VS. ANGELS

10TH INNING, 6-6, VS. JARROD WASHBURN
Ortiz hits a walkoff home run to left-center field to complete the series sweep. "When I walked to the plate, I was thinking, 'Let me try to get this over with.' I reviewed all the at-bats I had against him and [figured] he might want to try to get me out with the cutting fastball. So I went looking for it, and he threw it to me, and I got it."

2004 ALCS, GAME 4 VS. YANKEES

12TH INNING, 4-4, VS. PAUL QUANTRILL
Walkoff, two-run home run into the Yankee bullpen ends a 5-hour, 2-minute game and gives Red Sox hope after they had lost the first three games of series, including a 19-8 debacle one night earlier. Ortiz's two-out, two-run single in the fifth inning off Orlando Hernandez had given the Red Sox a shortlived 3-2 lead.

2004 ALCS, GAME 5 VS. YANKEES

14TH INNING, 4-4, VS. ESTEBAN LOAIZA
On the 10th pitch of the at-bat, Ortiz fights off a ball in on his fists to drop a single into center field that scores Johnny Damon from second for Ortiz's second consecutive extra-inning walkoff hit. In the last of the eighth inning, Ortiz had homered off Tom Gordon to bring Boston within 4-3.

2004 ALCS, GAME 7 VS. YANKEES

FIRST INNING, 0-0, VS. KEVIN BROWN
With two outs and Ramirez on first after Damon had been thrown out at home plate, Ortiz blasts a two-run homer to give the Red Sox a critical early 2-0 lead on their way to a 10-3 victory and the first comeback from a 0-3 series deficit in baseball history.

2004 WORLD SERIES, GAME 1 VS. CARDINALS

FIRST INNING, 0-0, VS. WOODY WILLIAMS
Ortiz kicks off the World Series with a one-out, three-run home run to get the Red Sox on the board and off to an auspicious start. He added an RBI single in the bottom of the seventh to help the Sox establish a 9-7 lead, but the Red Sox squandered both leads before Mark Bellhorn homered for the victory.

2007 WORLD SERIES, GAME 3 VS. ROCKIES

THIRD INNING, 0-0, VS. JOSH FOGG
Ortiz doubles to score Jacoby Ellsbury with the game's first run, then comes around to score on Mike Lowell's single as the Red Sox continue their momentum from winning Games 1 and 2 in Boston. They win Game 3, 10-5, and complete the sweep the next night, as Ortiz again scores Ellsbury with the first run on an RBI single in the 4-3 win.

2013 ALCS, GAME 2 VS. TIGERS

EIGHTH INNING, LOSING 5-1, VS. JOAQUIN BENOIT
With the Sox having lost Game 1 and shown little offense in Game 2, the series – and the postseason – turned when Ortiz hit a line-drive grand slam into the bullpen on the first pitch he saw from Benoit to tie the score at 5-5. The Red Sox earned the walkoff win an inning later, then won three of the next four games to take the series, 4-2.

2013 WORLD SERIES, GAME 4 VS. CARDINALS

FIFTH INNING, LOSING 1-0, VS. LANCE LYNN
Trailing in the game and 2-1 in the Series, Ortiz doubles and scores the first Red Sox run of pivotal Game 4 on Stephen Drew's sacrifice fly after giving the team a scorching pep talk between innings. Ortiz went on to go 3 for 3 with a walk, and also scored ahead of Jonny Gomes on Gomes's deciding three-run homer. The Sox swept the final three games for their eighth world title.

-RON DRISCOLL

MR. PERSONALITY

BIG PAPI // THE LEGEND AND LEGACY OF DAVID ORTIZ

Ortiz holding a fan's baby during the national anthem before an August 2013 game at Kauffman Stadium in Kansas City; Previous page: Leading the way to the Marathon finish line at the 2013 rolling rally.

EVERYBODY LOVES DAVID

BY JOHN POWERS

The nickname came from his being the new guy in Fort Myers. "I couldn't remember anybody's name," David Ortiz recalled. "So I called everybody 'Papi' because that's what they do in the Dominican. It's just a friendly thing, a sign of respect. After a while they started calling me 'Papi' in return and then it became 'Big Papi.' It took off."

Only a few seasons after Ortiz arrived in Boston he no longer needed a last name. Big Papi was plenty. There was a Big Papi plane, a sandwich, and a hot sauce. Was there anyone who didn't know of him, he was asked after only two seasons here. "A child that was just born today?" he guessed puckishly.

Ortiz's size, smile, and style made him universally recognized and revered. "He's the most charismatic baseball player I've ever been around," said Yankee's designated hitter Alex Rodriguez, who called him "a big cartoon character." "Whites like him, blacks, Hispanics, everybody. Everybody loves David Ortiz."

Particularly those who knew him best – his teammates. "Personality-wise, the way he carries himself, the way he goes about his business, he's a true professional," pitcher Jon Lester once said. "From Day One that I've been here, he's never changed...You can't ask for anything more as a teammate than having David Ortiz in that locker room with you."

Papi's daily arrival in the clubhouse was an entrancing event. "The way that he talks, the way that he walks into a room, all eyes turn to him," said Red Sox manager John Farrell. "Not just because of his stature and what he's accomplished but the energy and life and fun-loving approach he has for the game and a certain situation."

Ortiz's tenure alone (14 seasons in the Fens) gave him patriarchal primacy. "Daddy's back," declared catcher Christian Vazquez when Ortiz turned up for his final spring training. When Boston won the World Series in 2013, Ortiz was the only man remaining from the fabled 2004 club and was treated as an oversize oracle. "If this guy wants to rally us together for a pep talk it was like 24 kindergartners looking up at their teacher," said outfielder Jonny Gomes.

He might not have been the captain, but Ortiz had a customized role. "I have three different jobs here," he said. "1. Designated hitter, 2. Cheerleader, and 3. Make sure that we have everything stay where we like it to be."

Because he appeared for only a handful of minutes in every game, Ortiz's mere emergence from the dugout was an occasion marked by possibility and puissance. "How many players in the game do you stop to watch him swing the bat?"

> ## "YOU CAN'T ASK FOR ANYTHING MORE AS A TEAMMATE THAN HAVING DAVID ORTIZ IN THAT LOCKER ROOM WITH YOU."
>
> **– JON LESTER**

mused Yankee second baseman Robinson Cano. "When you think of the Red Sox you think of him."

Ortiz was the gargantuan, gregarious, and grinning face of the franchise. "He brings a great spirit and sense of humor and a big, bear-like personality to the park," observed club president Larry Lucchino. "He leads the league in hugs."

Nobody made an entrance like Papi, garbed in skintight urban finery and Diesel shades and bedraped in diamonded bling from earrings to watches to wristbands to "DO 34" chains. "Best-dressed All-Star every year," said Orioles outfielder Adam Jones. "Not even close."

That style, which included muscle cars like the red Mercedes-Benz convertible that was his quarter-million-dollar present to himself after the 2004 title year, was what Ortiz called "how we roll."

So when his Minnesota teammates wanted to play a prank on him during an exhibition game, they filched his clothes, leaving him to cram-jam himself into a county worker's orange jumpsuit. "You should have seen him," said Doug Mientkiewicz, who later became Ortiz's teammate in Boston. "The suit was up to his shins. There were buttons popping off all over the place. He came over to our clubhouse yelling and hollering. That's an image I will never forget."

Big Papi always was a supersize special edition, the only one of his kind on the shelf. Bodacious, bedazzling, and beloved. "I've never heard one bad thing said about David Ortiz," said Sox second baseman Dustin Pedroia, "and I don't think I ever will."

A selfie on the South Lawn with the president in April 2014; a hug for Nomar after Garciaparra's three-run homer in September 2003; a dapper David receives the 2011 Roberto Clemente Award at the 2011 World Series.

In his hometown of Santo Domingo in January 2010, where a donation was made to the David Ortiz Children's Fund to support youngsters who need treatment from Heart Care Dominicana.

THE GUY BEHIND THE SMILE

BY AMALIE BENJAMIN

When David Ortiz enters a clubhouse, he strides in confidently, almost dancing. He looks as if he owns the world and, at this moment, perhaps he does.

He says this is who he is. He is the man with the smile, joking and yelling and grinning all at once. His personality reaches out, into the stands, through the TV, across a table. He says it in his clothing choices – the man prefers matching shirt-and-cap combos that are often about as loud as his voice.

"I think everybody pretty much knows what it's all about [with] me," Ortiz says. "I don't like and I don't believe in people who are pretty normal when everything is going well and they change when they see a bump in the road. I let them know straight up I don't like it. That's the way I am. I don't like lies. I don't like two faces. I don't feel comfortable with it. I'll tell you what

A celebratory splash courtesy of Hanley Ramirez after his extra-inning double beat the Astros in a May 2016 game; with Xander Bogaerts, helping to send Derek Jeter into retirement in 2014.

I feel in a heartbeat. That's me."

David Ortiz, on the field and off, does not hide.

That's part of the reason why the slugger was one of the most popular players in baseball, part of the reason why, only 2½ seasons after the Minnesota Twins decided he was not worth re-signing, Ortiz received more votes than any other player for the 2005 All-Star Game, picking up 4,138,141, including more online tallies than anyone else.

It's why he is beloved. Ortiz was never the enigma that Manny Ramirez was. He didn't have the stoic, no-nonsense persona of Jason Varitek. He wasn't confrontational and dramatic, except in his flair for producing the game-winning hit. Ortiz is what he is.

The only question is what made him that way.

Because Ortiz isn't smiling now. He isn't grinning, isn't shaking. He's sitting, simply, and pain washes through his eyes. He's talking about his mother and about how, since the accident, nothing can get him down. Because nothing, he says, will ever be quite so hard.

Angela Rosa Arias was killed in a car accident in January 2002. It

was, absolutely, the most difficult moment in his life.

"At that point I have to be the stronger [person] in the family because, pretty much, my sister, my aunt, my uncles, my pop, pretty much everybody got hit really bad," Ortiz says. "I had to act like, 'Hey, let's hang in there.' I got to take the heat. I lose my mother, that I love, the person that give me the most love ever. But I never quit. I act strong in that one moment that was terrible. But I've got my pain. I deal with the situation. After that, I don't think I have faced anything worse than that, anything more painful than that.

"That's why I see everything in light and happiness."

This isn't the Ortiz of the ballpark. This isn't the Ortiz of the commercials, the ones that show him gregarious and laughing. This is the other David Ortiz. The one that he keeps inside.

"Life is a challenge," Ortiz said. "Life is a challenge that you need. There's things in life that are going to throw you into the ground, but if you learn how to get up, that means you are not a quitter. That's the best that a human being can have, never quit. If you quit, if you are a quitter, you're giving up on your kids, your wife, your family, you're giving up on them."

He says he's never done that, never given up, though he came close after his mother died. He won't, he says, if he hasn't yet.

He has taken that pain and transformed it into joy. It has been subsumed into the old Ortiz, the one before he lost his mother and lost his job in Minnesota almost at the same time. It was the one that started before and blossomed after, once the sorrow became less

acute and life got, well, good. Even in a city as notoriously tough on its talent as Boston, Ortiz stayed Ortiz.

"I don't think the environment has anything to do with his personality," said Terry Ryan, Ortiz's general manager with the Twins. "If you go down to the Dominican, he's the same there. He's the same in Boston. He did the same in Appleton, Wis. He's always had a smile. He's got a flair about him. He's got a charismatic approach."

It isn't just his personality, of course. Ortiz has done more than enough at the plate to satisfy the legions of Red Sox fans who adore him, more than a few of whom walk around with his name branded across their backs. Ortiz has simply been transcendent in the playoffs through his career, often getting the hit at just the right time.

Ortiz effectively won the World Series for the Red Sox with his bat in 2004 and in 2013. And, just for that, he could be deified in Boston. In this town, his swings mean just as much as his smiles.

"If he stunk and he hit .150 and hit zero home runs and drove in nobody, people wouldn't have that," said Varitek in 2005. "The fact [is] that he's extremely good at what he does, one of the best in the game and he has that very likable persona. When you're mechanically sound, as he is, those slumps are short. That's what makes him so good."

He was good – and reliably consistent. Ortiz hit .287 or better eight times in his first 13 seasons in Boston, and he hit 30 or more home runs nine times in those 13 seasons.

"ORTIZ SWAGGERS INTO A CLUBHOUSE WITH A SMILE AND JOKE, A ONE-MAN MERENGUE FULL OF NOISY HAPPINESS AND DELIGHT, READY TO DRILL HIS NEXT VICTIM WITH A FOUR-LETTER LINE DRIVE TO THE FUNNY BONE."

– KEVIN PAUL DUPONT, BOSTON GLOBE SPORTSWRITER

A long time ago, when Ortiz was little, his father explained baseball to his son.

An escalator, he said. You rise with it, getting on when you reach the big leagues. Each step is an achievement: playing well, making the All-Star team, winning a World Series. He dreamed of winning a Most Valuable Player award as the final step in that progression, but the closest he came was in 2005, when he finished second. It appears that he will have to settle for "Most Popular."

"He went from being a good player to one of the elite hitters in the league," said Terry Francona, Ortiz's manager for eight seasons in Boston, from 2004 to 2011. "And then you add on his infectious personality, his ability to smile. He has the quickest, warmest smile I've ever seen. He can make a person who walks through that door he's never met before feel so comfortable. And that is a gift. You couple that with his ability, you have David Ortiz."

Ortiz sits, thinking quietly in a clubhouse normally filled with thumping rhythms. His father slightly shorter, slightly rounder, is behind him, 20 yards away. Ortiz, still not smiling, considers his answer.

Is he ever not, well, him?

"Of course, as a human you get down," Ortiz said. "Everything is not only happiness. Everything is not flowers and a piece of cake. There's a lot of things in life that you see, that you have to face. That's life. But, otherwise, happiness."

And that, really, is David Ortiz.

THE MAN

BIG PAPI // THE LEGEND AND LEGACY OF DAVID ORTIZ //////

Pausing during batting practice in July 2016. Previous page: Sharing a 2014 spring-training moment with son D'Angelo.

THE PLAYFUL,
PROUD FACE OF THE CITY

BY JOHN POWERS

I t was a black-Hispanic immigrant from the Caribbean who helped bring together a shattered place five days after the 2013 Boston Marathon bombings. "This is our [expletive] city and nobody is going to dictate our freedom," David Ortiz proclaimed during a tribute to victims, survivors, and responders at Fenway Park before the Red Sox played their first home game after the tragedy. "Stay strong."

He was born in Santo Domingo and came to America to play a child's game. But it only took a couple of seasons for Ortiz to become a baseball hero and a few more years to be a civic icon. So his defiant declaration became Boston's full-throated

response to a terrorist act. "What we've been through this week, that was my feeling," Ortiz said. "I was hurting like everyone else. That's how I am."

When the Dominican Republic was inundated with water in the spring of 2004, Ortiz put a cardboard box on a table in the Sox clubhouse. "Please, any help you can donate to the people of my country — D.R.," he wrote. "They got hit by the flood."

His personal generosity to charitable causes in both of his homelands is boundless. The David Ortiz Children's Fund, established in 2005, provides critical pediatric care, including heart surgery, for young patients in both countries. "You get famous and you have what you need, but sometimes there's always something missing," he observed. "Right now I feel I'm a full package."

If the cause involved children, Ortiz always was quick to step up to the plate. "I love to be a kid," he declared after spending an afternoon playing Wiffle Ball and munching loaded sausages with 30 of them to fulfill a $30,000 auction donation to benefit Good Sports, a Dorchester nonprofit that gives sporting goods to city kids.

Papi's perennial playfulness in and out of uniform made him a cherished character hereabouts. When he became a U.S. citizen in 2008 it was a significant and symbolic story. "It's a great country," said Ortiz, whose wife and children were born in the States. "Proud to be here, now proud to be a part of it."

From the start, Ortiz and Boston embraced each other with open-armed affection. He was a symbol of the social transformation of the city, playing for the last ballclub to integrate in a tribal town that was being riven by racial unrest when he was born. Big Papi is a bilingual ambassador who's as comfortable in a Hyde Square barbershop as he is at City Hall, where he and the former Hizzonah were best buddies. "That's my man, you know," Ortiz said of the late Tom Menino. "Me and Menino, we go way back."

If Menino held the formal title, Ortiz was the unofficial mayor, eternally affable and approachable. In 2013, when he was named Most Valuable Player as the Sox won the World Series for third time in less than a decade, he finished third in the mayoral race with more than 500 write-in votes.

"I remember John Henry once told me that I was the only player he's ever known who really is able to play in Boston," Ortiz remarked. "And he's right. I know how to handle everything in Boston."

He was comfortable in a town that had great expectations of its ballplayers but faint memories of them delivering championships. That changed when Ortiz led the resurrection against the Yankees that led to the breakthrough 2004 title and established him as a civic colossus.

"This is as close a bond between a player and the city in the game of baseball," Sox president Dave Dombrowski mused early in 2016. "When you talk about what he accomplished, what the team accomplished, his ability and his length of time here, very few guys mean that much to this city."

Ortiz could have set down anywhere after the Twins cut him loose because his price was going up. He chose the city on a hill that had never seen anyone quite like him. "My life, I've been built up around this organization, this city, and these fans," Ortiz said. "The best thing that ever happened to me was to come play in Boston."

Joining Boston mayor Marty Walsh in helping five-term former mayor Tom Menino throw out the first pitch on Opening Day 2014; preparing for Game 1 of the 2013 World Series as a rainbow splits the sky.

Ortiz greets Diana Reyes, 12, who was born with a hole in her heart, after Ortiz's fundraising efforts helped to provide for surgeries for her and other indigent children in the Dominican Republic.

A HEARTFELT GESTURE

BY STAN GROSSFELD

In January of 2006, David Ortiz was preparing for the baseball season in his hometown of Santo Domingo. Unlike previous seasons, there was a special urgency for the Red Sox slugger; as a member of the Dominican Republic national team, he knew his participation in the World Baseball Classic would cut into his spring training. There was no time for distractions.

But one day he took a break.

"My friend says, 'Hey, let's go to this one place, I just need five minutes from you,'" Ortiz recalled.

And that request helped save the life of 12-year-old Diana Reyes, who was born with a hole in her heart.

Dr. Fred Madera, a surgeon with the Heart Care Dominicana Foundation, which was established to aid indigent children with congenital heart disease, will never forget Big Papi's visit.

"He showed up [at the Hospital General de la Plaza de Salud in Santo Domingo]," Madera said. "He saw kids with purple lips and purple nails, because of a lack of oxygen. He started talking to the parents. 'Hey, you like baseball?' They said, 'Yeah, but my kid has never been able to play. He's gasping for air.'

"Then [Ortiz's] eyes got watery. This huge guy was very touched."

Ortiz saw a dozen kids that day. One wore a Red Sox cap and said his dream was to play baseball, but he couldn't.

"Ortiz noticed he was big," said Madera. "He said, 'That could be me.' He kind of wiped his tears — he cried. I thought, 'Hmmm. This big guy, I didn't know he had tears.' He said, 'Well, you're gonna play baseball,' and he signed a baseball."

Ortiz also saw a child who had just come out of surgery.

"He learned how one child's illness affected the whole family," said Nelvea Pelaez, executive director of Heart Care Dominicana. "The social impact is more than fixing a hole in the heart of one kid.

"We had to take him out. He had this look on this face — not looking at anybody, just gazing at the horizon. All he said was, 'I have to do something about this. I'll be back.'"

Less than a year later, Ortiz kept his promise and returned with a check for $200,000, enough to start the first pediatric cardiovascular unit in the Dominican Republic.

"When I saw David go into the intensive care unit, I didn't see a big star going in there," said Pelaez. "I saw someone letting their real feelings come through. When you see that, you say, 'Oh my God, this is an original — not like a politician or a movie star.'"

Ortiz isn't embarrassed to ac-

Ortiz visits with children and parents at the Hospital Generalde la Plaza de la Salud in his hometown of Santo Domingo after presenting a check for $200,000 to Heart Care Dominica in 2006.

knowledge that he cried.

"Yeah, I get a little bit sad about it," he said. "It hurt my feelings. When you see a child that needs help and you know if you make a move, you can make it happen . . .

"I went back to the States and started working [on raising money].

"Baseball is not everything in my life. I have a lot of things I worry about, just like I worry about baseball. There's some people out there struggling badly.

"I'm telling you, a bad day at the field is not even close to what they go through. A bad day on the field, you can replace it the following day. Sick people, a sick kid, there is no way to replace that until somebody makes a move to help the children out.

"I think of a bad day at the field

> "IT IS BEAUTIFUL TO GIVE A CHILD BACK HER LIFE. IT'S SOMETHING PRICELESS."
>
> **– JACQUELINE REYES,** WHOSE DAUGHTER, DIANA, WAS BORN WITH A HOLE IN HER HEART

and a good day at a hospital. The good day at the hospital can make your whole year. That's the way things seem like to me."

Nearly 1 percent of children born in the Dominican Republic have some sort of birth defect that requires surgery. Because there is no pediatric cardiac hospital in the country, sometimes a US team of surgeons, in a mission of mercy, will save a few kids in a nation in which more than 1,000 children are in need. Few can afford the $40,000 operation in the United States. In the Dominican, the operation costs $5,000.

But Ortiz came through in the clutch again.

"We've already operated on four children thanks to David Ortiz's sponsorship," said Dr. Pedro Urena, president of Heart Care Dominicana, who studied at Brown University. "Some of the rooms are still under construction."

There are more than 600 children on the Heart Care Dominicana waiting list. "Sometimes they call a family and say, 'Bring your kid in,' and there's this silence and the mother says, 'I wish you called last month, our girl has died,'" said Pelaez. "That's when you have to go on rounds and look at the faces of the kids that you fixed; otherwise, you won't do it anymore."

Reyes was one of the first to benefit from Big Papi's generosity. She was the only one in the still-being-constructed patients' room when Ortiz toured the facility earlier this month. She had a doll, a heart-shaped red pillow, and a smile that lifted everybody's spirits.

Ortiz, who has a natural way with kids, was impressed.

"She was really happy and excited about seeing me," said Ortiz. "She

was thanking me for what I did. When she was thanking me, I was like, 'No, don't thank me, thank New England. Thank the Red Sox and those fans that donated money.'"

The Red Sox Foundation matched funds, and fans, corporate sponsors, and players made up the rest. Ortiz says for him, it's easy.

"The athlete has the capacity to collect money," he said. "I'm really excited about what I'm doing and I'm going to keep on doing it as long as I can."

Recovering in the new cardiovascular unit in the pediatric wing of the hospital known as CEDIMART (Centros de Diagnostico y Medicas y Telemedicina), Reyes acknowledged that she had never seen Big Papi play; she only knew him from commercials and billboards. For this event, the media were out in full force. Ortiz also met the Dominican first lady, Margarita Cedeno de Fernandez, to discuss the plight of Dominican children. She called him a "true ambassador."

Ortiz, looking stylish in a black sports jacket, red shirt, red shoes, designer sunglasses, and turquoise earrings, first visited a packed room with sick kids. It will be the intensive care unit when it is finished. There he signed the oversized $200,000 check.

"Hopefully everything keeps going and the children get better," he said. "Everything is looking good and I see a lot of happy faces out there. God bless you guys."

Then he visited Diana's room.

"I was frightened at first, he's so big," said Diana. "But he was very nice. Afterward I felt so wonderful. He resembles the poor people, the real people. I'll be grateful forever. I'll pray every day that he hits more home runs."

When Big Papi kissed her twice, her eyes lit up brighter than the lights of Estadio Quisqueya, where the local stars play.

She said it was the first time she was kissed by a boy. A very big boy.

Ortiz chatted with her and signed some baseballs for the nurses. Then he was whisked off to the Red Sox Academy near Santo Domingo, where a batting cage was named in his honor.

"What David Ortiz has done for us is something that we never could pay back," said Reyes's mother, Jacqueline, who works on a textile assembly line for $31.58 a week — barely enough to support Diana, buy her medicine, and feed her two baseball-crazed siblings.

"It is beautiful to give a child back her life. It's something priceless. God bless him wherever he is. It's a miracle."

Ortiz says for him, it's a natural thing. His charitable fund-raising seemed to increase after the death of his mother in a car crash in the Dominican Republic in January 2002.

"It comes from my parents, my mom and dad," Ortiz said. "They teach me how to do the right thing. I tried to keep it with myself. Now everybody looks at you like a role model. I don't feel that I am.

"People are needing help and, basically, if you can afford to do something to help somebody out, I don't mind."

In December of 2006, Diana Reyes got to go home, where all the relatives were waiting. She was greeted like Big Papi at home plate after a walkoff home run.

"We celebrated," said Jacqueline Reyes. "I was jumping up and down."

Not surprisingly, Ortiz speaks his mind when he addresses fans during a pre-game ceremony honoring the victims of the Boston Marathon bombings, five days after the attack. "We had never been through what we went through the past week," he said later.

'THIS IS OUR [EXPLETIVE] CITY'

BY JULIAN BENBOW

The emotions had been boiling all week.

A five-day stretch that had been frantic and unsettling had come to an end. So had the search for the suspected perpetrators of the bombings that shook the city not even a week earlier.

Looking out at the faces in the crowd that April day in 2013, people who had come to Fenway Park to escape, to celebrate, and recapture some of the normalcy they had lost, David Ortiz felt what they were feeling.

"This past week, I don't think there was one human being who wasn't affected by what we got going on down here," Ortiz said. "This past week for me, myself, I was very emotional and angry about the whole situation and got to get that out of my chest and make sure our fans and everyone in the nation knows that this is a great nation and part of it was supporting each other when everything went down."

At the end of the ceremony that preceded the Red Sox' 4-3 win over Kansas City, Ortiz's microphone was hot and his words were clear:

"This is our [expletive] city, and nobody is going to dictate our freedom. Stay strong."

He later apologized for the swear, but not the sentiment. But in the wake of incomprehensible terror, the words were forceful, defiant, and proud.

"I'm from the Dominican Republic and the one thing that I always say is me and my family are blessed by being in this country," Ortiz said. "And I love this country and I would do anything for this country. Everybody was one unit and that's what matters."

Preaching the mantra "Boston Strong," the Red Sox took the first steps in helping an embattled city to heal. The team's support added to the solidarity the city had shown all week in the face of tragedy.

Governor Deval Patrick said, "The response of the people in the crowd in the stadium has been the response of people all over the Commonwealth all week and, frankly, all over the world."

Over the course of the pregame

Ortiz's words became a rallying cry, as evidenced six months later when he homered in Game 1 of the World Series; becoming a U.S. citizen in a June 2008 ceremony at the JFK Library.

ceremony, emotions swung from moment to moment.

A montage played on the outfield scoreboards, image after powerful image.

"That video was pretty moving," Sox manager John Farrell said. "When you consider all that has transpired from the celebration of someone finishing a marathon to the devastation that followed that to all the video, if you watched TV the last 36 hours, I think it was all captured in that five-minute video."

Marathon volunteers lined the Green Monster in front of an American flag as wide as the 231-foot long wall.

Ken Shiff and his wife, Beth, were both starting-line volunteers.

They spent the morning of the marathon meeting the elite athletes, talking with runners. Once they were done, they went to the finish line to cheer their friends.

"And then the whole world changed on us," Ken said.

Standing against that wall, they said they felt unified.

"It's so important," said Ken, 59, a Methuen native. "We've been through hell and back to get through this week. And just to come here and be united with all these people who have the same feelings that we have and to know that it's all over and it's all safe again . . ."

Beth, 60, his wife of 37 years, finished his sentence, "It was just amazing."

The Royals and Red Sox stood shoulder to shoulder along the foul lines.

"Guys were fighting back tears on the line," said Sox reliever Andrew Bailey. "I've never been a part of something like that."

For the national anthem, the crowd of 35,152 became a choir, singing all together.

The field was flooded with the faces they had seen endlessly on television over the past four days. Patrick, Boston Police commissioner Edward Davis, and FBI special agent Richard DesLauriers. They joined marathoners Rick Hoyt and his father, Dick, longtime symbols of the sacrifice and resilience, who threw out the

ceremonial first pitch along with off-duty firefighter Matt Patterson and bombing victim Steven Byrne.

Thinking about pitching was almost impossible for starter Clay Buchholz with everything unfolding in front of him.

"I don't think I would've been able to watch it and pitch at the same time," he said. "That was my frame of mind going in. That's the part that I wanted to get through."

One minute everyone in the ballpark was silent, remembering the victims. The next they were applauding the heroes in front of them on the field.

"Then a baseball game breaks out," Jonny Gomes said.

"EVERYBODY WAS ONE UNIT AND THAT'S WHAT MATTERS."

— DAVID ORTIZ

To be able to play, the day after a manhunt left the city all but frozen, was a statement in itself. The scene at Fenway Park on that Friday had been surreal.

"It was just weird to look out the window and not see any action, not see any cars, see any people," third baseman Will Middlebrooks said. "It was like a ghost town. Everyone was on lockdown. It was pretty scary to know I was a couple miles away. I'm just happy it's over."

There were signs of change.

Security was heightened. Earlier in the day, police dogs checked the ballpark. Officers in bright yellow jackets seemed to be at every turn. Fans were wan-

ded down at the entrances.

But there were signs that the day obviously meant more.

It took a 4:30 a.m. flight for Neil Diamond to make it to Boston from Los Angeles. Then, he called into the main Fenway Park switchboard and asked if he could sing "Sweet Caroline." The crowd was his choir.

As much as it meant to come away with the win, everyone understood that there was a bigger victory in just being there.

"I wanted to win this game today badly," Ortiz said. "I've had a lot of great moments and emotional situations. Today was different. We had never been through what we went through the past week."

THE LEGACY

BIG PAPI // THE LEGEND AND LEGACY OF DAVID ORTIZ //////

A two-run homer in July 2016 against the Rays brings a familiar finish. Previous page: Fans walk past a watchful Papi on Yawkey Way.

TO GO WHERE NO DH HAS EVER GONE

BY JOHN POWERS

T he definitive legacy for all ballplayers is to reach the Hall of Fame, and while his team-mates dubbed him "Cooperstown" a while ago, David Ortiz won't find out for at least five years whether he'll join the roster of his sport's bronzed immortals. If elected, Ortiz would become the first designated hitter and only the third native of the Dominican Republic (along with Juan Marichal and for-mer teammate Pedro Martinez) to be enshrined.

While his career numbers clearly measure up (no DH ever has posted better), the essence of Papi's legacy is what he did when the moment beckoned. "I don't do anything but go out there and hit once in a while so I've got to get people to know me," he once observed. "The best way to get people to know me is to produce at the right time."

The right time is October and only three other men, all Yankees, have hit 500 home runs and earned three World Series rings. Babe Ruth, Mickey Mantle and Reggie Jackson played for a dynasty where winning the Fall Classic was considered a birthright. Before Ortiz arrived in the Fens in 2003, Boston hadn't produced a championship since 1918 and had reached the playoffs only six times since 1975. With him at the plate they did it six times in the next seven years and earned two rings.

Much of the difference was due to Ortiz's dramatic knack for extending autumns with one swing. "I've never cried at a baseball game before but I couldn't help it," admitted owner John Henry after Ortiz had driven in the winning runs against Oakland and kept alive the 2003 season – his first with the team.

There was a Ruthian sense of anticipation whenever Papi stepped into the box with a big game on the line and, as often as not, a Ruthian result followed. "I always back it up," Ortiz said. "As long as I've been playing here I've been backing it up."

Since he gave up playing first base on an everyday basis in 2005 and was paid simply to leverage lumber, Ortiz only had a handful of chances per game to deliver, often with men on base. "Hitting is hard, bro," he'd say.

Ortiz did his damage even when rivals lopsided the diamond against him with shifts or wouldn't throw him a strike, preferring to pitch around him, even with slugger Manny Ramirez on deck. "Every year there's something new to

54

HOME RUNS
IN 2006,
ESTABLISHING
A FRANCHISE
RECORD

148

RBIs IN 2005,
FOURTH-MOST
IN RED SOX
HISTORY

Clockwise from below: Keeping the faith that sight unseen, a ball will get signed at spring training 2005; admiring the flight of a three-run blast in 2003; a young fan from Atlanta opts for the red jersey; battering the Yankees in 2003.

figure out," he said. "Every year they find another way to pitch me and I've got to make adjustments.... It never ends, man."

Yet much of Papi's production came after he was 35, when he made the All-Star team four times. "He's still performing at this level all these years later," former Boston general manager Theo Epstein, who signed Ortiz off the street, said after he hit his 500th homer in 2015: "Amazing."

Some skeptics questioned how the same man that the Twins gave up on at 27 could transform himself into one of the game's greatest bashers. While Ortiz's name was leaked in 2009 as one of nearly 100 major leaguers who tested positive for performance-enhancing drugs in a 2003 confidential screening, Commissioner Rob Manfred came to Papi's defense in October 2016. Manfred noted that there were at least 10 false positives in the survey testing, adding, "I think it's really unfortunate that anybody's name was ever released publicly." Manfred confirmed that Ortiz has never failed a test since MLB implemented its drug policy in 2004. Ortiz maintains that he is baffled by the positive result from 2003.

The only thing that figures to keep Ortiz out of Cooperstown is if voters conclude that his statistics were chemically amplified. "If one day I'm up for the Hall of Fame and there are guys who don't vote for me because of that, I will call it unfair," Ortiz said.

The larger practical and philosophical question is whether Ortiz will be able to overcome the traditional balloting bias against DHs, who play in only one league and rarely wear a glove. But in the Hub and elsewhere Papi's legacy has more to do with his sorcery than his statistics. "I would like people to say when they see me walking by: 'There's the guy who made the impossible become possible,'" he said.

"PEOPLE NEED TO UNDERSTAND THAT WE ARE HUMAN. WE'RE NOT SUPERHEROES. WE HAVE THE SKILLS TO PLAY A SPORT NOT MANY PEOPLE ARE ABLE TO, BUT THAT DOESN'T MEAN WE'RE FROM ANOTHER PLANET. SOMETIMES THINGS COME OUT AND I'LL THINK BACK AND WISH I HAD SAID IT ANOTHER WAY. BUT I DON'T REGRET IT. NEVER."

— DAVID ORTIZ

Clockwise from left: Ortiz checks out the latest hat of a devout fan in 2013; Boston Marathon bombing survivor Patrick Downes, backed by the Achilles Freedom Team, throws out the first pitch to Ortiz in April 2016; adding ring No. 2 in 2007; Hall of Fame numbers and names adorn the ballpark.

LOVE
EVERLASTING

BY DAVID FILIPOV

I t might seem wildly off base to suggest that an event in mid-July of 2016 demonstrated David Ortiz's unprecedented status among iconic Boston athletes, given the Red Sox slugger's already teeming résumé of clutch, franchise-altering October performances.

Moreover, it had little to do with Ortiz's statistically historic season for a 40-year-old — an emphatic exclamation point at the end of a Hall-of-Fame-worthy career.

No, it was something that happened before a game on July 19, a day when the nation was reeling from a wave of racially charged violence. Boston police officers, elected leaders, and clergy had assembled on the field at Fenway Park for a moment of silence. But when the announcer called on "our leader, to whom we have turned so many times when the chips were down," it was Ortiz who stepped up to the mike.

His message — "Let's be kind to each other, and choose love" — wasn't as profound as the confirmation it represented of Ortiz's

Clockwise from right: Stalwart Sox fans ceaselessly back Papi; his pregame liner gets lodged in the Pesky Pole in July 2016; throwing out the first pitch with fellow Boston icons Bobby Orr and Bill Russell on Opening Day 2016.

role as a civic leader.

And that, more than anything, indicates why Big Papi has a chance to figure more prominently in Boston after he plays his last game than other local sports legends have.

In this city, the biggest superstars tend to avoid the spotlight when the stadium lights go down. Carl Yastrzemski only reluctantly makes appearances; Larry Bird says he still loves Boston, but we seldom see him when the team he runs, the Indiana Pacers, isn't playing here; Bill Russell and Boston kept each other at arm's length for decades until a recent rapprochement; Bobby Orr, who has handled the glow of retirement as well as anyone, is a distant enough memory that young hockey players have trouble recognizing him.

> ### "HALL OF FAME PLAYER AND A HALL OF FAME PERSON. THAT'S THE BEST WAY I CAN PUT IT. YOU LOOK AROUND THE GAME AND DAVID IS THE LEADER. HE BRINGS PEOPLE TOGETHER."
>
> **— ADAM JONES,** ORIOLES' OUTFIELDER

But Ortiz goes out of his way to make waves. When, in the wake of the Boston Marathon bombing, Ortiz punctuated his exhortation to a city scarred by terror by shouting an expletive on live TV,

the Federal Communications Commission didn't censure him, it applauded him.

Ortiz is not the only local sports hero to make an important contribution outside the lines — he's not even the greatest Red Sox hitter to do it, not in a world that included Ted Williams, who served in two wars and tirelessly campaigned on behalf of the Jimmy Fund.

Speaking of the Splendid Splinter: Ortiz, while nowhere near as foul-tempered as Williams, has occasionally come off as petty when grumbling about the official scorer or complaining about his contract. Williams was a first-ballot Hall-of-Famer; Big Papi's worthiness as a candidate for baseball's most venerated shrine has been the subject of debate, in no small part because of the allegation of performance-enhancing drug use that he has never cleared up. Another thing regarding Williams: Ortiz refuses to believe that Teddy Ballgame really hit a ball 502 feet, to a spot in the right field bleachers marked by a red seat, a target Papi has been unable to reach, even while taking aim in batting practice.

Where Ortiz tops Ted is the seemingly limitless enthusiasm with which he embraces his role as an all-star ambassador.

It came out July 18, 2016 at a gala for his charity, which raises money to help children in New England and his native Dominican Republic get access to critical pediatric care. Ortiz spoke, without notes, and "had the audience eating out of his hand," according to the Globe's Red Sox beat writer, Peter Abraham.

It came out again two days lat-

er, when Ortiz played cheerleader-in-chief during Boston's 11-7 defeat of San Francisco. Big Papi high-fived and hugged the hero of the game, the oft-maligned Hanley Ramirez, jumping up and down on aching, aging feet and legs with an oversized smile, like a father at a Little League game.

It comes out in the little moments before games, when Ortiz chats amicably in Spanish with stadium employees who call out from the seats, or jokes with a woman on crutches about their respective leg ailments.

It helps Ortiz's legacy that his last season is full of moments when he backed up his supersized persona with legendary feats on the field. There was the time in April when he told a sick child he was going to hit a home run for him and then did it.

There was the time he defied the elements in a July 19 game, the night of his "Choose love" speech. In his first at bat, Ortiz hit a ball that died on the warning track, knocked down by a ferocious wind. On his way back to the dugout, Papi pointed an accusing finger into the breeze, as though issuing a challenge to Aeolus himself. His next at bat, with his very next swing, Ortiz drove a 442-foot laser out of the park, a three-run home run that figured prominently in a 4-0 Red Sox win.

Two days later, while launching his usual array of bombs in batting practice, Ortiz hit a ball so hard it got stuck in the metal grill of the right-field foul pole, 302 feet away. The pole bears the name of Johnny Pesky, another beloved Red Sox luminary, whose failure to throw the ball in a critical 1946 World Series moment is the only dent in his armor; Ortiz is so strong that the ball he unleashed put a dent in Pesky's Pole. Then he hit another home run in the game, a 13-2 Red Sox win.

Ortiz is a superstar, but he's not invincible. When he came up with the bases loaded, no outs, and his team down by a run in the bottom of the ninth the next night, he grounded into a double play and the Sox lost.

Ortiz is ultimately beholden to the rule of "win some, lose some," just like any Boston sports great. Except some of the ones he's won have reversed curses and uplifted an entire city. Which, as much as anything he does with his charity and his dazzling smile after he retires, is why we'll remember him long after the games are over.

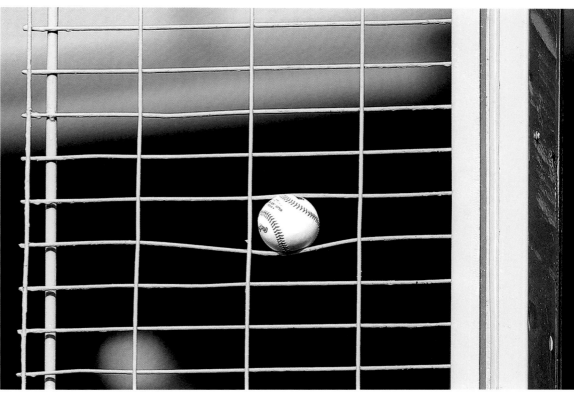

Clockwise from below: Hugging daughter Alex, 15, after she sang the national anthem on Opening Day 2016; waving the AL pennant flag in 2013; a family of Papi backers waits to cross Boylston Street; Rod Carew, a Hall-of-Fame hitter, greets Ortiz before a July 2016 game.

MITSUBISHI ELECTRIC

Boston
Scientific NESN FUEL

34

FINAL SEASON

BIG PAPI // THE LEGEND AND LEGACY OF DAVID ORTIZ

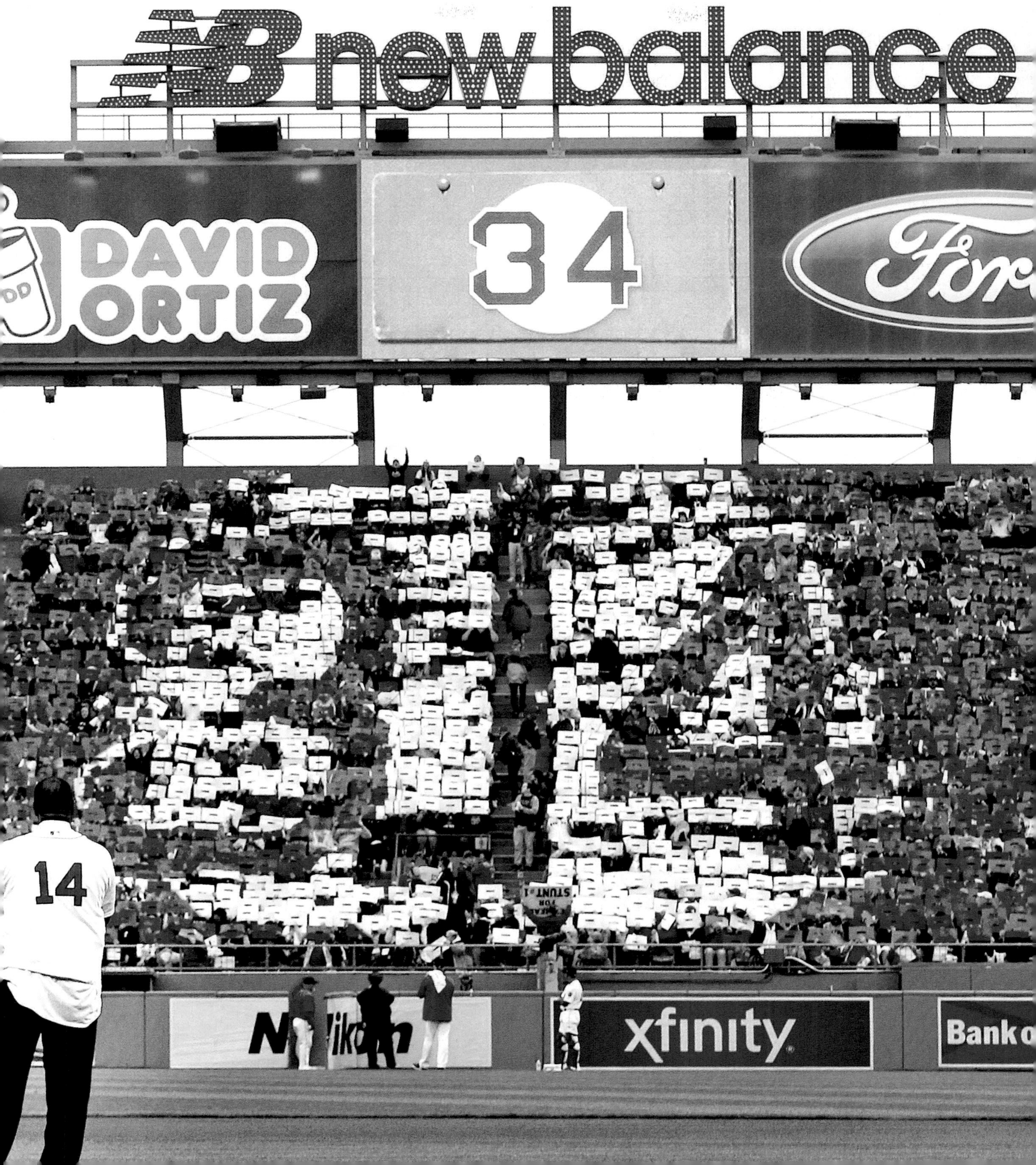
new balance
DAVID ORTIZ
34
14
xfinity

Ortiz celebrates a first-inning homer vs. Colorado in May. Previous page: Ortiz's No. 34 is displayed by bleacher fans holding cards as it is announced that the number will be retired in 2017.

A NATION SAYS
THANKS

BY JOHN POWERS

David Ortiz knew before the previous season ended that he had only one more left in him. His body felt the accumulated mileage every day. "It's not an easy game to play when you're my age," he said. His rare stint standing sentinel at first base for nine innings stiffened him up like the Tin Man. Even his designated hitter duties required him to arrive at the ballpark by noon for a 7 p.m. game, to limber up. Increasingly, there were more days off to let his sore legs rest and recuperate.

After 19 major-league seasons and a career filled with achievement and honors, Ortiz decided that it would be prudent to retire a bit sooner than later. "I see so many players going out not on their own terms," he mused. "That doesn't look right to me. I think people respect you more if you can do it the way you want."

So on Nov. 18, 2015, his 40th birthday, Ortiz declared that his 20th season and 14th in Boston would be his last. "This is it," he said in a two-minute video. "It was a chapter in my life and I want to go on to the next one. I don't want to be the guy that people feel sorry for."

His valedictory was a hail and farewell that ran from February into October, with his teammates especially motivated to extend it into November. "We're trying to get to the World Series every year," second baseman Dustin Pedroia said during spring training. "But there may be a little added something to get David there one more time. How cool would that be, right?"

Along the way to autumn there were tributes to Ortiz in every city where he was making his final appearance, frequently with charitable donations and almost always with customized keepsakes. A cable-car bell from the Giants. A Stetson cowboy hat from the Astros. Boots emblazoned with BIG PAPI from the Rangers. A surfboard from the Padres. A handmade humidor with 50 Davidoff cigars from the White Sox. There were a Hublot watch and 34 pounds of salmon from the Mariners, his

original club, plus a framed copy of his first professional contract. The Twins supplied a 64-ounce jar of peanut butter, recalling a prank by former teammate Corey Koskie. The Orioles gave him the remains of the dugout phone that he'd shattered with his bat three years earlier, after striking out.

And the Yankees presented him with a leather-bound collection of personal letters from his pinstriped rivals present and past. "Some players are born to be Yankees," Ortiz wrote to them. "I was born to play against the Yankees."

Yet, this was no King for a Day tour. Ortiz still was in the lineup, batting third or cleanup and contributing percussive punctuation to the most remarkable final season in baseball annals. He batted .315, his best number since 2012. His 38 homers and 127 runs batted in were his most in a decade and set major-league records for players 40 and over, as did his doubles (48) and extra-base hits (87).

Papi's final lap was marked by Ruthian moments, beginning with a homer in his final spring training at-bat. After promising a 6-year-old boy from Cheyenne with a congenital heart defect that he'd hit a home run for him that night, Ortiz hammered a two-run blast to beat the Yankees. "It was God putting his hands on a baseball player," he declared. Then he belted two shots in the Bronx on Mother's Day. "I know she's in a place just watching me," said Ortiz, who ritually looked skyward and pointed both index fingers after crossing the plate, an image that was mowed into the Fenway outfield for the final home series.

In mid-May, after a homer in the third inning and a game-tying triple in the ninth, Ortiz banged a two-out offering for a 420-foot double off the wall to beat the Astros in the 11th. "Just say I'm a bad [deleted]," he proclaimed after the first double-triple-homer outing of his career.

Even batting practice was a must-see event. Before a July date with the Twins, Ortiz drilled a ball so hard that it was wedged in the Pesky Pole's metal screen. "He puts on a display every day," marveled manager John Farrell. "We're watching history right in front of us, nightly."

Only Ted Williams, who at 42 hit .316 and launched 29 homers, the last in his final at-bat, had gone out with more drama. Williams, though, was playing for a seventh-place club in 1960. Ortiz was a centerpiece of a pennant contender that was bidding to become a remarkable worst-to-first-to-worst-to-first story.

In the second half of September when the Sox won 11 straight against the Yankees, Orioles, and Rays to clinch a playoff spot, Ortiz hit .410 with 13 runs batted in and four homers. The most prodigious of them was a two-run, first-inning, game-winning blast at Tampa Bay that struck the catwalk above the rightfield stands more than 400 feet away. "I felt goose bumps," said first base coach Ruben Amaro Jr.

When the club returned to Fenway for the final weekend of the regular season, Ortiz was feted with a trio of pre-game celebrations that left him both exhilarated and exhausted. "It was unbelievable," he said. "I wasn't expecting so much... Everything went better than perfect. It was very special."

Before the Sunday finale against Toronto, when teammates from the three championship clubs turned up bearing the World Series trophies and Dominican Republic president Danilo Medina threw

IN 2016, DAVID ORTIZ SET SINGLE-SEASON RECORDS FOR PLAYERS AGE

40
OR OLDER WITH

48
DOUBLES,

87
EXTRA-BASE HITS,

38
HOME RUNS, AND

127
RBIs

> "IMPRESSIVE, MAN. THERE WAS NO BOOING OUT THERE. IT SEEMS LIKE EVERYONE WAS HAPPY THAT I'M LEAVING."
>
> **— DAVID ORTIZ,**
> ON THE OVATION HE RECEIVED IN HIS
> FINAL GAME AT YANKEE STADIUM

him the first pitch, Ortiz was presented with a $1 million donation to his Children's Foundation from the Red Sox Foundation and the club's limited partners.

The Sox announced that they would retire his number next season. Governor Charlie Baker said that the state had named the overpass between Kenmore Square and Fenway Park the David Ortiz Bridge, and Mayor Marty Walsh announced that the walkway between the ballpark and the Yawkey commuter rail station would be David Ortiz Drive. "Any time you get bridges and roads named after you, you've obviously got one hell of a legacy," Farrell observed.

The legacy that Ortiz and his teammates most wanted, though, was a fourth ring. "The last day of his career I want to see him holding a trophy and crying," said first baseman Hanley Ramirez. "That is my goal. I want to see him cry. That is the best present we can give him."

NOTE: THIS BOOK WENT TO PRESS AT THE CONCLUSION OF THE 2016 REGULAR SEASON.

Clockwise from far left: Before his final regular-season game, Ortiz remembers his late mother, Angela; he reacts as Governor Charlie Baker and Boston Mayor Marty Walsh dedicate roadways to him; and teammates past and present fete his exploits, including the 2004 World Series he won with Pedro Martinez.

Clockwise from right: Ortiz holds USA gymnast Aly Raisman's Olympic medals so she can throw out the first pitch in August; Papi celebrates in New York on Sept. 28 after the Red Sox were assured of first place; Xander Bogaerts cools Ortiz down after Papi went 4-for-4 vs. the Indians in late May; he congratulates Mookie Betts after Betts's first-inning homer against the Twins in July.

Ortiz and
Maverick
Schutte, 6,
of Cheyenne,
Wyo., work
on their
celebration
technique as
Maverick visits
Fenway Park
in May.

A HOME RUN FOR MAVERICK

BY RON DRISCOLL

Maverick Schutte's mother makes it very clear that Red Sox Nation has an outpost in Wyoming. "We're a Red Sox family," said Marti Linnane, whose husband, Mike, is a Portsmouth, N.H., native. "We were married in our Red Sox jerseys. We always watch the games together – it's Maverick's favorite thing to do. We love the Red Sox."

But Maverick is not your average 6-year-old. He is being treated at Denver Children's Hospital and has spent much of his life there. On April 29, 2016, Maverick was having a tough

"YOU TALK ABOUT SUPERHEROES? HE'S A HERO TO BE ABLE TO GET THROUGH ALL THE TOUGH TIMES."

– DAVID ORTIZ

day, so former Red Sox player Kevin Millar, a longtime supporter of the Children's Miracle Network Hospitals, tried to cheer him up.

Before the Red Sox-Yankees game at Fenway Park, Millar filmed a video with David Ortiz to wish Maverick well. Ortiz went even farther, promising that he would hit a home run for Maverick that night.

"When he saw the video he jumped on top of me and hugged me and said, 'This is the best day of my life.' He wouldn't go to bed; he had to watch the game," said Marti. "When David hit the home run, it was such a thrill. We knew why it happened."

Ortiz's "called shot" – the 507th homer of Big Papi's career – was not just any long ball. It came off the Yankees' Dellin Betances, one of the best relievers in the game. Ortiz had been 0 for 7 with four strikeouts against him before the homer, a two-run shot in the eighth inning that won the game, 4-2, for the Red Sox.

When Ortiz hit the home run, he did not remember his promise until he crossed the plate and saw Millar in the stands with his children and pulled them close for a group hug. Later, Ortiz said, "I think God is the one who takes over this stuff."

"Maverick just knew David was going to do it," said Marti. Before Maverick finally went to bed, he sent a video to Ortiz via Millar.

"Big Papi, you never let me down and you're the best player ever in the Red Sox game and I'm trying the hardest to get out there to Fenway Park and meet you," said Maverick, who has undergone more than 30 surgical procedures and has survived heart failure.

"It was very touching," said Ortiz. "I started thinking about it when I got home. That was when I really was like, 'Wow, I can't believe this really happened.'"

Less than two weeks later, on May 11, Maverick thanked Big Papi in person at Fenway Park, where it didn't take him long to feel at home. Maverick talked with Ortiz and several other players in the clubhouse before being interviewed in the Red Sox dugout, where he playfully took the microphone and conducted his own interviews.

"You're talking about 6 years old and he's been through hell," said Ortiz of Maverick, who wore a Red Sox cap, an Ortiz jersey and Batman Crocs. "You talk about superheroes? He's a hero to be able to get through all the tough times."

"Every day you bump into people complaining about life. When you see things like this, you have to thank God every day for being able to wake up and be healthy."

> "YOU EXPECT IT. IN THIS GAME IT'S SO TOUGH TO DO, AND HE MAKES IT LOOK EASY."

— DUSTIN PEDROIA, ON ORTIZ'S GAME-WINNING HOMER VS. TORONTO ON SEPT. 30

Clockwise from far left: Mookie Betts and Ortiz go airborne to celebrate Ortiz's final home run, on Sept. 30 at Fenway vs. Toronto; avoiding a foul ball in May; taking a knee and doffing his cap to the fans before his final regular-season game; hanging with Hanley Ramirez at the season opener in Cleveland.

Clockwise from right: A seventh-inning stretch message for Ortiz in his regular-season finale; amid the hoopla, a swing and a miss; a young New Hampshire fan hopes for eye contact; Ortiz steals second after his game-winning double vs. the Astros in May; Fenway fans can't believe their hero is signing off. Previous page: Preparing for a mid-September game vs. Baltimore.

AN INSIDE LOOK

AT DAVID ORTIZ'S LAST MOMENTS IN A RED SOX UNIFORM

David Ortiz came back onto the field to salute the crowd one last time following the final game of his career, a season ending Boston loss to Cleveland.

BY ALEX SPEIER

David Ortiz arrived at Fenway Park early Monday afternoon aware that it might be his last day as a player. For the first time in his career, he circled the ballpark in his car, trying to grasp the full dimensions of the potential finality.

A player who over the season's final months typically eschewed batting practice in favor of time in the trainer's room made a point of popping out of the dugout and into the cage before Game 3 of the American League Division Series. By his third round of hacks, he was launching comets over the Red Sox bullpen as if as a final offering of gifts to the fans.

He could not deliver the same in the actual game. Indeed, he did not have the opportunity to do so.

That Ortiz's final plate appearance — bottom of the eighth, chance to tie a playoff game with something of an echo of his famous home run against the Tigers in 2013 — should feature four straight pitches off the plate, en route to a walk and an eventual departure in favor of a pinch runner, seemed too anticlimactic to stomach, even for Ortiz.

"Once I got out of the game, I was screaming at my team to put me back in it," Ortiz said of his transformation into a cheerleading role at 9:21 p.m. "Make me wear this uniform one more day, because I wasn't ready to be over with the playoffs."

Yet the choice didn't belong to Ortiz or to the sold-out crowd at Fenway Park that wanted to see the 2016 season prolonged by at least another game.

And so, when the Red Sox' 4-3 defeat against the Indians was complete at 9:51 p.m., tens of thousands refused to leave.

Perhaps it was a state of disbelief after 14 seasons in which Ortiz continually breathed life into his home park ("We want Pa-pi"). Maybe it was simply the hope that this franchise giant would accept one final bow ("Thank you Papi"). But they remained.

Manager John Farrell spoke to a somber Red Sox clubhouse, and Ortiz followed. His career over, the substance of Ortiz's message nonetheless heralded his excitement for the future of the organization.

According to Xander Bogaerts, Ortiz said to "just be optimistic and be proud of what we achieved. Obviously, with all the young guys coming up, we have a

lot of potential. He's looking forward. He sees what the future has in stock and he definitely appreciates that for this organization."

SPEECHLESS IN THE SPOTLIGHT

That message delivered, Ortiz learned that the fans remained. And so, just over 10 minutes after the conclusion of the game, he walked back onto the field, encircled by photographers, and headed to the pitcher's mound — close to where he made his declaration of defiance on behalf of Boston in 2013.

This time, there was no speech, only freely flowing tears and the last gesture of a cap raised out of respect to all who were there, in all corners of the park.

"Tonight when I walked to the mound I realized that it was going to be — it was over," said Ortiz. "It was pretty much the last time as a player [to] walk in front of a crowd. And the emotion came back out.

"I've been trying to hold my emotions [the best] I can, but that last second I couldn't hold it [any] more. That's how we feel about what we do, because we love what we do.

"I respect this game so much and I love this game so much that as long as I played, I wanted to always be one of the best — not because of me, not because of my personal stats, because I don't really care about that. I really care about the fans. I really care about the emotion that they live through."

Those sentiments — and tears — were reciprocated from the stands.

By 10:08, he'd returned to the clubhouse and stood alone at his locker for a moment, head sunken, before disappearing to the shower area. After a few minutes, he ruptured the silence, bellowing praise to his teammates for their accomplishments in making the worst-to-first pivot.

By the time he emerged to the main locker room at 10:29, Ortiz was once again beaming, jovial both in the company of his teammates and at the sight of his son, D'Angelo, and his father, Leo.

"Dude, I've got to take a picture with my dad!" Ortiz exclaimed boyishly.

Red Sox mental skills coach Bob Tewksbury approached Ortiz with a copy of a picture from 19 years earlier, when the two sat in the Twins dugout. On Sept. 2, 1997, Ortiz made his big league debut as a pinch hitter in the pitcher's spot for Minnesota against the Cubs. The Twins starter in that game had been Tewksbury.

"He said I was there in his first game when he got called up and I was there for his last game," said Tewksbury.

Ortiz asked Tewksbury to show the picture to his father, then the slugger took a picture of the two men together. Others — players, security guards, clubhouse attendants — continued to approach Ortiz to express their admiration and affection. Finally, just after 10:30 p.m., Ortiz adjourned from the clubhouse into the interview room.

"*Ultima vez,*" he chuckled as he entered to visit with reporters.

Last time.

A BRIDGE AND AN EXIT

The press conference alternately connected with the worlds that Ortiz bridged, the player serving at times as his own translator, immersing himself in both languages to such an extent that, at one point, he absent-mindedly offered an answer in his second language to an inquiry presented in his first.

When the word "psyche" was mentioned, Ortiz asked for a definition of it. He later used the word in an answer. That facility in his second language served as a reminder: This outsized personality became so familiar only because he took it upon himself to master a language other than his native tongue.

Given the scarcity of bilingual reporters covering the Red Sox for publications in New England, Ortiz very easily could have been an icon for one culture but a relative unknown to another. Thanks to his own initiative, that was not the case. In his second language, he revealed more than many players have in their first.

"I can't ask God for any more than what he gave me," he said. "I'm a guy that came out of the Dominican one day when . . . I just turned 17 years old, and all I want to do was have fun at what I do.

"And then through my career I saw a lot of things happen. I saw a lot of guys being lost in their life, not just their career, but their life in general, because this is everything that they have and they never made it.

"And everything that I saw that cut them short, to not make it in their career, I kind of played it out like it was myself.

"Viewing things from the outside, [keeping] my feet on the ground and trying to learn through the process and not taking anything for granted [gave] me a 20-year career.

"That kid that was expecting just to have fun, here it is, 23 years later, having a career and walking home.

"I'm happy and proud of going home the way I am right now."

A few minutes later, Ortiz's press conference concluded. Exit stage left.

"*Que te vaya bien,*" pronounced MLB senior vice president Phyllis Merhige, the press conference moderator.

Fare thee well.

At 11:44 p.m., nearly two hours after the end of Ortiz's career, a few dozen loiterers dotted Van Ness Street, hoping for one more glimpse of the man. Inside the white SUV that left the players' lot, a wave came from a silhouette. Those last fans responded in kind, raising their hands as they watched the shadow of a legend disappear into the night.

David Ortiz bids a bittersweet fond farewell to the Fenway faithful after the Game 3 loss.

THE NEXT STAGE

BIG PAPI // THE LEGEND AND LEGACY OF DAVID ORTIZ

David Ortiz spoke emotionally about his experience since being shot in the Dominican Republic.

'I WOULD WAKE UP FEELING LIKE I'M GOING TO DIE'

BY BOB HOHLER

It was painless at first, the bullet that ripped through David Ortiz's torso and lodged in his friend's leg.

"I felt a burning sensation," Ortiz told the Globe in his first public comments to an English language publication since he was shot June 9 in his native Dominican Republic. "I felt weird, like not myself, as I went down."

The former Red Sox great had been sipping Scotch with seven or eight friends at a familiar hangout, the trendy Dial Bar and Lounge in Santo Domingo, and was chatting with a singer known as Secreto when a gunman rushed his front row table at the bar's outdoor patio and fired a single bullet from close range into his back.

It was a moment, Ortiz said, that has forever changed his life.

In a wide-ranging interview at Fenway Park, Ortiz reflected on the crime and investigation, the lifesaving Samaritan who rushed him to the hospital, his three surgeries and potentially deadly infection, and how differently he views the world now.

"People need to understand, this isn't a movie where you get shot in the street and you're back two minutes later," Ortiz said. "No, I got shot and almost died. I only have one life to live. I can't just go to the pharmacy and buy another one."

As a grainy videotape of the shooting shows, Ortiz slumped to the bar's wooden floor within seconds of the gunshot. It was about 9:20 p.m., more than two hours after he had arrived there to meet Jhoel Lopez, a Dominican television host, and a longtime friend, Sixto David Fernandez, who operates a car paint shop.

At the sound of the shot, patrons scattered, including Ortiz's companions — even the wounded Lopez. Ortiz was left alone, writhing on the floor, critically injured.

"Then this angel comes out of nowhere," he recalled.

> # I GOT SHOT AND ALMOST DIED. I ONLY HAVE ONE LIFE TO LIVE. I CAN'T JUST GO TO THE PHARMACY AND BUY ANOTHER ONE.
>
> — DAVID ORTIZ

The angel, a Dial Bar patron named Eliezer Salvador, helped Ortiz into the back seat of his Rolls-Royce SUV. The vehicle was boxed in by other parked cars, so Salvador rammed his way out of the space, sending Ortiz rocking back and forth in his seat.

They sped toward a public hospital, only to change course when Ortiz asked to be taken to a private clinic he had frequented. He remained upright and conscious as Salvador, who once had been shot in the stomach himself, weaved at a harrowing pace through traffic.

"He knew how to react," Ortiz said. "He kept talking to me to make sure I stayed awake."

The 43-year-old retired slugger remembers being alert enough to know he had been shot, but he understood little else about his wound or condition.

"I didn't want to look at it, to be honest," he said. "I don't even remember how much I bled."

He does recall, however, when the pain set in: in the half hour it took the clinic staff to evaluate and prepare him for the operating room, and then wait for the surgeons to arrive.

As he was rolled into surgery, Ortiz said, he told the staff, "Please don't let me die. I have four children. I want to be with them."

Doctors operated on his badly damaged intestines and liver, and removed his gallbladder. By morning, the Red Sox had arranged to transport him to Massachusetts General Hospital.

Before he left, Dominican Attorney General Jean Alain Rodriguez questioned him at his bedside about the shooting. This would be his only interview with a law enforcement official about the ambush, according to Ortiz spokesman, Joe Baerlein.

"Everything happened so fast that it felt like it didn't happen," Ortiz said of the interview. "But it really did."

While Ortiz remembers speaking with Rodriguez, he recalls little else about the day after the shooting except asking his father, Leo, who accompanied him on the flight to Boston, to cover his feet when they grew cold.

"The next thing I knew I was being wheeled into surgery again" at Mass. General, he said.

Dr. David King, a renowned trauma surgeon, told Ortiz he needed to operate to assess the damage and the quality of the first surgery.

"They did a hell of a job, all good," Ortiz quoted King as saying afterward about the Dominican surgical team.

But his recovery was arduously slow. Then, three weeks after the second surgery, Ortiz encountered another life-threatening crisis: an acute bacterial infection that gravely compromised his digestive system. His fever ran so high that he shook with chills, as he had as a child when he suffered hypothermia.

The doctors and nurses, for all their reassurances, did not mask the severity of his condition.

"It was very dangerous," Ortiz said. "I got to the point that I started losing hope."

Ortiz grew more despondent when he learned he urgently needed another surgery. He remembered seeing fear on the faces of his loved ones.

"Everybody was like, 'Oh [expletive],'" he said.

In his bleakest days after the surgery, Ortiz fought desperation, even in his sleep. Over seven weeks, he could swallow nothing but melted ice chips — except for a small cup of Jell-O and some fruit that he threw up.

Ortiz drew his only nourishment through tubes and intravenous lines. His mouth was so parched that it ached.

"I had nightmares all the time about being in the desert, looking for water," he said. "I would wake up with my mouth dry and feeling like I'm going to die."

Ortiz drew a measure of hope when the medical team would tell him he would survive. But he began to prepare for the possibility that he would be permanently debilitated, that he would never again be Big Papi, the robust and charismatic personality whose spirit had long lifted those around him.

"I felt that if I didn't die, then I would never be the same again," he said. "I went through hell with that."

One day, Ortiz awoke from a nightmare and saw his sister, Albania, seated by his bed, her Bible open on her lap. He had tubes in his nose and arm. He had lost 40 pounds.

"She was arguing with God, asking for help," he said. "It was upsetting. It hit me hard."

Looking back, however, Ortiz sees that moment as his turning point. It would take several more days for him to eat and drink again, and to speak without struggling to his wife, Tiffany, and family.

"But after that day, everything was different," Ortiz said. "I started getting better."

On July 22, nearly seven weeks after he was gunned down, he held down food for the first time: a cup of soup. The fever was gone. The feeding tube had been removed.

"That was a big, big deal," he said.

Ortiz was no stranger to Mass. General. Through his charity, the David Ortiz Children's Fund, he has given millions to Mass. General and other medical facilities in the United States and the Dominican Republic to help critically ill children.

His stay at the hospital was long and grueling but also heartening. "They made me feel special there," he said, "but when I noticed that they treated everybody like they treated me, that made me even happier."

Nearly a month after his third surgery, Ortiz returned to his home outside Boston, beginning the next phase of his recovery. Walking, eating, sleeping in his own bed, spending time with friends: It all felt renewing.

The Yankees came to visit: CC Sabathia, Edwin Encarnacion, Luis Severino, Gary Sanchez. The Phillies, too: Jean Segura, Maikel Franco. Also, the Red Sox, past and current, if not in person then by phone.

But nothing has fully distracted him from the mystery of why that stranger emerged from the shadows in Santo Domingo that night with malice and a firearm. To date, nothing about the conflicting findings of Dominican law enforcement has made sense to him, Ortiz said.

First, the authorities announced that an unspecified person with an undisclosed motive had placed a $7,800 bounty on Ortiz's head. Six suspects were arrested, and Ortiz said he knew none of them or why anyone would want to harm him.

"I don't know why I was involved in something like this because I'm not the type of person who looks for trouble or causes trouble. All I worry about is trying to help people, about trying to do the right thing," Ortiz said.

What's more, he joked: "You gotta pay a lot more than that to get me killed. I ain't that cheap."

Nearly three weeks later came another announcement. Eight more suspects had been arrested — Ortiz said he knew none of those, either — and police concluded that the actual intended target had been his friend, Fernandez, who sat near him that night.

The bounty on Fernandez was closer to $30,000, authorities said, and his cousin, an alleged drug dealer, had wanted him killed because he allegedly had spoken to

Clockwise from right: Support for David Ortiz from the Red Sox community was overwhelming, including the team flying him from the Dominican Republic to Massachusetts General Hospital; Ortiz deeply appreciated the medical care he received and embraced the second chance at life.

police about him more than eight years earlier.

This also made no sense to Ortiz. Now, there are questions about whether Cesar Peralta, a Dominican drug kingpin known as "The Abuser," or his cartel may have been involved in the shooting, which to Ortiz also defies logic.

Ortiz also dismissed tabloid rumors that have emanated from social media in the Dominican Republic. One suggested a car he was driving had been chased and forced off the road by someone trying to harm him before the shooting.

"If that ever happened to me, the first person I would call would be the president of the Dominican Republic," Ortiz said. "I know he would do something about it. That's how close we are."

Last month, Ortiz hired for-

mer Boston police commissioner Ed Davis to investigate the shooting. Baerlein said Davis has yet to uncover any significant new evidence.

"I want to find out who did this," Ortiz said. "I'm not going to sit around and chill if there's somebody out there who wants to kill me."

Ortiz now looks much like his old larger-than-life self, if a little more svelte. He has gained some weight back and seems to move freely, saying he recently logged a 5-mile walk. But the shooting has made Ortiz adjust his lifestyle; sadly, he said, he finds himself withdrawing a bit.

"I like to embrace people, make them feel comfortable around me," Ortiz said. "I was always very accessible, but I think I'm going to cut down on that a little now."

"One lesson I've learned is that you can't be naive," he said. "There are a lot of things going on now that you have to be aware of. I need to pay attention and be more careful."

Ortiz expressed thanks to Red Sox Nation and other supporters, and said through his spokesman that he was touched by how generous and kind people have been to him and his family. He is also particularly grateful to John W. Henry and his wife, Linda Pizzuti Henry, who facilitated his emergency medical flight to Boston. Henry is the principal owner of the Sox and the owner and publisher of the Globe. Pizzuti Henry is the Globe's managing director.

The Henrys recently flew David and Tiffany Ortiz to southern France, where they vacationed on the couple's yacht, toured a vineyard, and sampled a bottle of wine so extravagant that Ortiz jokingly speculated it was drawn from "the fountain of youth."

When they returned, Ortiz made his first big public appearance, tossing a ceremonial first pitch at Fenway Park and soaking in the affection.

He plans to leave soon for Los Angeles to resume his role as a Fox Sports analyst for the major league baseball playoffs in October. Then comes a November trip to Florida for his annual charity golf tournament. One day, he said, he will return to the Dominican Republic, likely with security.

By Thanksgiving, Ortiz said, he expects to be fully recovered, at least physically. He knows other scars will linger.

WE WELCOME ALL
VISITORS WITH DISABILITIES.
PLEASE LET US KNOW
IF WE CAN
BETTER SERVE YOU.

DAVID ORTIZ HAD A PRESENCE IN THE HALL OF FAME. NOW, HE'LL BE IMMORTALIZED

BY PETER ABRAHAM

The hallways of the National Baseball Hall of Fame and Museum were nearly empty on a cold January morning. The only sound was a gentle tap-tap-tap in the Plaque Gallery, where a custodian was repairing a loose baseboard.

There is a reverential aura in the room, almost as if talking loudly would disturb Babe Ruth or Ty Cobb. But come July, there will be more of a celebration with David Ortiz at its center.

Ortiz is headed for the Hall of Fame, the announcement coming Tuesday night that he was the only player elected by the Baseball Writers' Association of America.

The Red Sox icon is scheduled to be inducted July 24. At the age of 46, Ortiz is now a baseball immortal.

Fittingly, Ortiz's plaque will be placed on the well-varnished oak walls of the gallery approximately 20 feet from that of his former Red Sox teammate and good friend Pedro Martínez.

The Hall of Fame has been collecting — and displaying — Ortiz memorabilia for years, cataloging a selection of bats, uniforms, spikes, and other keepsakes that suddenly have considerably more meaning and value.

Ortiz, who told the Globe last week that he has never visited Cooperstown, is eager to get a look.

"I know it's a special place," he said. "As a player, you try not to think about the future too much.

Following his 2000th career hit – one of many major milestones in his Hall of Fame career – David Ortiz acknowledges the ovation from the crowd.

But the Hall of Fame is the ultimate."

That Ortiz just cleared the required 75 percent — he received 77.9 percent — is the story for now. It won't be for long.

Joining Martinez, Wade Boggs, Carl Yastrzemski, and Ted Williams as the only Red Sox players to achieve first-ballot status ultimately will be what's remembered, as will Ortiz becoming just the fourth player from the baseball-crazed Dominican Republic to gain entrance to Cooperstown.

"That means everything to me, representing my country like that," he said.

A vast majority of voters understood that the story of baseball in the 21st century couldn't be told without Ortiz as a main character. It's a Hall of Fame, after all, and who's been more famous than Big Papi in that time?

Ortiz may not be the best player in Red Sox history, but he is surely the most impactful, given his outsized role in three championships, particularly with the historic 2004 team.

With the Sox trailing, three games to none, in the American League Championship Series against the rival Yankees, Ortiz won Game 4 with a home run in the 12th inning. A day later, his single in the bottom of the 14th inning won Game 5.

The Sox never lost again that October. Ortiz drove in 19 runs in 14 games during that postseason.

"If I had to say what was the biggest thing, it was winning in 2004," Ortiz said. "A team like the

Red Sox went 86 years with no championships, and we did it. Everything changed after that."

Ortiz also helped comfort a bomb-scarred city in 2013, leading the Sox to a cathartic championship. He retired a few years later, still one of the most feared hitters in the game.

Now comes the diamond-studded cap on his career.

"The Hall of Fame, it's something you learn about when you're a kid," Ortiz said. "It's like a storyteller talking to you about a superhero type of thing.

When people talk about the Hall of Fame to me, that's how I feel. You're telling me a story about superheroes."

Ortiz's career was a marvel. He had 541 home runs, 632 doubles, 10 All-Star selections, and finished in the top five of the American League MVP voting five times.

Among players with at least 50 career postseason plate appearances, Ortiz's 1.372 OPS is a World Series record. In all, he hit .289 with a .947 OPS in 85 postseason games.

"We all know what he did on the field. That stuff's easy to see. You can look it up and see all the numbers," said Jon Lester, a teammate for nine seasons and two titles. "But to take on the role of a leader, not only in the clubhouse, but in that city — we all know how that city can be at times with just how hard they are and accountable that they make players.

"For him to do it day in and day out was pretty impressive to watch all those years."

Ortiz already has a significant presence in the Hall, and that becomes clear when you leave the plaque gallery and explore.

Over the years, the Hall has collected 13 pieces of Ortiz memorabilia — "3-D artifacts" in curator-speak — and much of it was on display before the voting results were announced.

Ortiz's jersey from the 2004 World Series hangs in the "Viva Baseball!" exhibit recognizing the vast impact Latin American players have had on the game.

Continue walking, and the spikes he wore at the 2016 All-Star Game during his final season are in a locker along with one of the commemorative baseballs used during the final regular-season game the Sox played that year.

A bat Ortiz used in the 2013 World Series is around another corner. Keep going and there are the spikes Ortiz was wearing in 2009 when he set the record for career home runs by a designated hitter.

Photographs or videos of Ortiz uncoiling his lefthanded swing are included in several exhibits, and he is one of the players featured in the 15-minute welcome film.

Go down some stairs and the Hall of Fame's vault reveals more treasures and a few frivolities.

There's a souvenir Ortiz watch the Sox gave away in 2006 along with an empty bag of "Big Papi's Tortilla Chips" and a bottle of wine he endorsed 16 years ago.

There's also the batting helmet Ortiz had on when he hit his 43rd home run of the 2005 season, setting a record for designated hitters.

The helmet is sticky with pine tar

and there's an inch-long crack on the side.

"I was going good that season and I kept using the same helmet," Ortiz said. "I probably threw it when I struck out and cracked it, but I kept on using it."

By 2013, as the Red Sox were in a playoff run that culminated with a championship, Ortiz's teammates temporarily nicknamed him "Cooperstown."

All he did that postseason was go 18 for 51 with 5 home runs and 13 RBIs in 16 games. Ortiz reached base safely in 19 of 25 plate appearance in the World Series.

By Game 6, the Cardinals gave up and walked Ortiz four times, three intentionally.

His career lasted three more seasons, but Ortiz's performance that October stamped his Hall of Fame passport.

"We called him 'Cooperstown' for a reason," teammate Jonny Gomes said. "He belongs there. I've never been around anybody like him before.

"In '13, he invited the entire team to his house every time we clinched something. Wives, kids, everybody. He had a way to connect with everybody in the room.

"He was pulled in so many dif-

Clockwise from below: With the announcement that he'd be inducted into the Hall of Fame, David Ortiz officially entered legendary status among Red Sox players; a closeup view of David Ortiz's handprints on the kids concourse at Fenway Park; with a permanent spot in Cooperstown, Big Papi's Red Sox legacy is complete.

ferent directions that season but always was as good as he could be on the field."

Ortiz's amplified personality can charm a toddler or the president. Without trying to be, he is inclusive.

In 2011, Mexican billionaire Carlos Slim, the richest man in the world at the time, had one request when he visited Fenway Park. He wanted to meet Ortiz.

"What's up, man?" said Ortiz, who startled the armed guards with Slim when he burst out of the trainer's room to say hello.

But Ortiz was a flawed protagonist at times. He was released by the Minnesota Twins after the 2002 season. The team decided he was not complete enough to merit a salary increase.

The Red Sox signed Ortiz to an inexpensive deal and made him earn playing time. Along the way, there were occasional bursts of anger di-

rected at umpires, opposing pitchers who brushed him back, and even his managers.

In 2009, Ortiz was identified in a report as having tested positive for a performance-enhancing substance in what was intended to be an anonymous survey six years earlier.

Ortiz denied taking anything other than over-the-counter supplements. He was deemed clean for 13 seasons after baseball started a testing program in 2004, which backed up that claim.

So did commissioner Rob Manfred, who said in 2016 that the 2003 test had discrepancies in how the results were recorded.

But suspicions and assumptions dogged Ortiz.

The Hall has never instructed voters on how to appraise the Steroid Era. But signs in the stately red-brick building near areas devoted to all-time records inform visitors that

the museum acknowledges steroids were part of the game, and the exhibits reflect that time.

Ortiz was primarily a designated hitter throughout his career, and that was a factor some voters held against him.

Lester blasted a hole in that argument.

"I think we've got to kind of get over that DH deal," he said. "I get it. I understand it. But it wasn't his choice. It's punishing somebody for having a position called designated hitter. I think that's unfair.

"In some of the biggest games, he played really good first base for the Red Sox. He would step in in the World Series for us at first base.

"I've never understood that argument. If you don't want to have that position, don't have the position available."

Ortiz also was shot and badly wounded on June 9, 2019, while at a bar in the Dominican Republic. Three surgeries and a six-week stay at Massachusetts General Hospital followed.

Officials in the Dominican claimed the shooting was a case of mistaken identity, an explanation that has invited skepticism but did not seem to affect his Hall candidacy.

It has been an eventful life, far more than he ever expected. Growing up, Ortiz liked to tinker with junk cars and thought his destiny was to inherit the auto-parts store owned by his father, Leo.

On Tuesday, with his father at his side, Ortiz was told he was a Hall of Famer.

"You have to pinch yourself," he said last week. "How did this happen to me?"

DAVID ORTIZ VISITS HALL OF FAME AHEAD OF INDUCTION IN JULY

BY PETER ABRAHAM

Until Monday, David Ortiz had never stepped foot in the National Baseball Hall of Fame and Museum.

It proved to be a day with a full count of emotions.

There was joy at seeing where his bronze plaque will be placed after he is inducted in July; awe at holding the bat Ted Williams used when he hit his final home run in 1960; and tears when he saw memorabilia related to one of his early mentors, Kirby Puckett.

"Here we are. Here we are," Ortiz said.

Ortiz was elected by the Baseball Writers' Association of America in January after a 20-year career that included 541 home runs and three World Series championships with the Red Sox.

With Hall of Fame vice president of exhibitions and collections Erik Strohl as his tour guide, Ortiz saw displays that highlighted Hank Aaron, Babe Ruth, the early days of the Red Sox, and some moments from his own career.

The plaque gallery made the deepest impression, as it does

Clockwise from far left: David Ortiz admires World Series rings from throughout the years; Ortiz took a tour of the Baseball Hall of Fame with Erik Strohl, the vice president of exhibitions and collections.

ORTIZ IS ONE OF SEVEN NEW HALL OF FAMERS SCHEDULED FOR INDUCTION ON JULY 24, 2022.

The preliminary trip to Cooperstown was a memorable one for David Ortiz and a great way to set the stage for the official ceremony on July 24, 2022.

with most visitors.

"Getting to know you're going to be part of where they are is something that is very impressive," Ortiz said. "Because I know what it takes for those guys to be where they're at.

"When you first begin, the last thing that you're thinking about is being part of that pack."

The Red Sox played an exhibition game here in 2005, but there wasn't time for the players to see the museum. Once Ortiz was elected, the Hall arranged for what it calls an "orientation visit."

With the surprised players from the baseball team at Easton (Pa.) High happily tagging along behind him and angling for selfies with the slugger, Ortiz took in the Hall and asked many questions.

A visit to the basement archives was particularly meaningful. Ortiz examined caps, gloves, spikes, bats, and other pieces of equipment from Ruth, Williams, Carl Yastrzemski, and other Hall of Famers.

When Strohl handed him a bat used by Puckett when he went 6 for 6 with two home runs on Aug. 30, 1987, Ortiz took a step back.

"My man. This was my guy," Ortiz said as he examined the black bat.

Ortiz explained that as a Minnesota Twins prospect in the late 1990s, Puckett took him under his wing. They remained close until Puckett's death in 2006, five years after he was elected to the Hall.

Later in the day, when recounting the moment, Ortiz paused and cried

for a few seconds before he composed himself.

"Once I saw his face on that plaque I started thinking about a lot of things," Ortiz said. "Then I tried to walk away but I got caught up . . . Kirby was a good friend to me. Kirby cared when I was just a kid — when I was nobody.

"I didn't know who I was going to be or where I was going to end up. He cared about me. That's what life is all about."

When Ortiz picked up a club-like bat used by Ruth, he started to swing and nearly clipped a shelf behind him.

"Be careful, Big Papi," Strohl said.

Ortiz also was impressed to hold the baseball from the final out of the 2004 World Series. The sacred sphere came into the Hall's possession in 2006 as a part of a settlement between the Sox and first baseman Doug Mientkiewicz as to who was the rightful owner.

"That's the one? Get outta here," said Ortiz, who hit .400 with five

> ## "OH, YEAH, THIS IS IT. WHEN YOU TALK ABOUT TED WILLIAMS, THAT'S EVERYTHING."
>
> **— DAVID ORTIZ**

home runs and 19 RBIs in 14 postseason games that year.

The Williams bat felt right in his hands.

"Oh, yeah, this is it," Ortiz said. "When you talk about Ted Williams, that's everything."

Ortiz is one of seven new Hall of Famers scheduled for induction on July 24. Former Minnesota Twins stars Jim Kaat and Tony Oliva were selected by the Golden Days Era Committee, which covered those from the years 1950-69, along with the late Gil Hodges and Minnie Miñoso. The late Bud Fowler and Buck O'Neil were selected by the Early Baseball Era Committee, for those whose contributions were primarily before 1950.

"It's going to be fun. I can't wait for that to happen," Ortiz said. "Just enjoy. It doesn't happen every day. I know it's a lot."

It will be a joyous day for Red Sox fans, too. Ortiz has come to understand that these last few months.

"I know the happiness that we bring to people," he said. "It's something I really cared about when I played. You hear people talking, especially in New England, about the game and the things that we do."

At the request of the Hall, Ortiz signed the spot where his plaque will be attached to the wall in July. It's a few feet away from his old rivals Mariano Rivera and Derek Jeter, and a section over from his friend Pedro Martinez.

"An amazing day," Ortiz said.

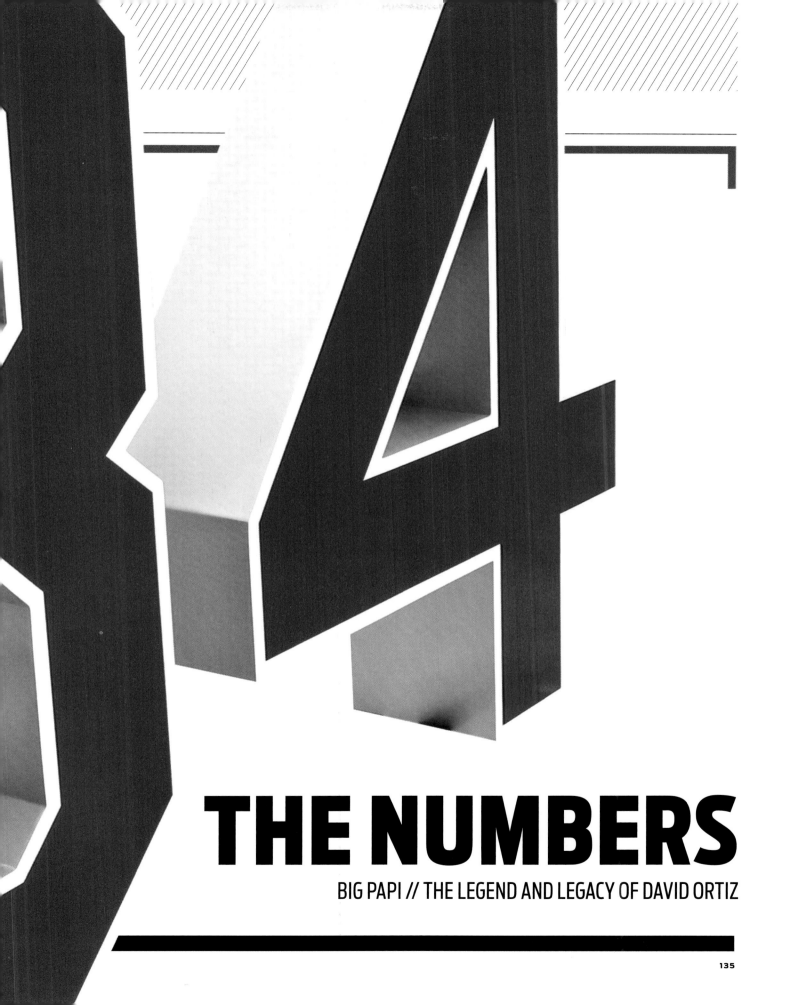

THE NUMBERS

BIG PAPI // THE LEGEND AND LEGACY OF DAVID ORTIZ

DAVID ORTIZ

MR. BIG

NAME: David Americo (Arias) Ortiz

NICKNAME: Big Papi (or Cookie Monster)

POSITIONS: Designated hitter and first baseman

BATS: Left

THROWS: Left

HEIGHT: 6' 3"

WEIGHT: 230 lbs.

BORN: November 18, 1975 in Santo Domingo, Dominican Republic

HIGH SCHOOL: Estudia Espaillat

DEBUT: September 2, 1997 (Age 21 – 14,750th player in MLB history)

HOME RUNS BY POSITION

- **3** PH
- **53** 1B
- **485** DH

BY RON DRISCOLL

David Ortiz finally gave up chasing Ted Williams. After trying to match it for years, Ortiz voiced his skepticism in 2015 about Williams's 502-foot home run in 1946, even though a lone red seat in a sea of Fenway Park green allegedly pinpoints where the blast landed. Knowing that the Splendid Splinter was revered in these parts as "the greatest hitter who ever lived," Big Papi found a way to forge his own Boston legacy: by winning.

Ortiz racked up glittering offensive numbers, to be sure, some of which eclipsed Teddy Ballgame, Carl Yastrzemski, Jim Rice, and others in the Red Sox pantheon. But the numbers that ultimately mattered most to Big Papi were the three world championships he delivered to a title-starved region that had not celebrated since long before Williams's time. Here are some facts and figures that help bring Ortiz's Fenway tenure into focus.

TRANSACTIONS

NOVEMBER 28, 1992: Signed by the Seattle Mariners as an amateur free agent.

SEPTEMBER 13, 1996: The Mariners sent Ortiz to the Minnesota Twins as the player to be named later in a trade for Dave Hollins.

DECEMBER 16, 2002: Released by the Minnesota Twins.

JANUARY 22, 2003: Signed as a free agent with the Boston Red Sox.

OCTOBER 30, 2011: Granted free agency.

DECEMBER 7, 2011: Signed as a free agent with the Red Sox.

OCTOBER 29, 2012: Granted free agency.

NOVEMBER 5, 2012: Signed as a free agent with the Red Sox.

CAREER MILESTONE HOME RUNS

100
May 28, 2004: A grand slam off Seattle's Joel Piniero at Fenway Park that gave the Red Sox a 6-4 lead on the way to an 8-4 victory.

200
June 29, 2006: A solo homer off the Mets' Duaner Sanchez in the eighth inning of a 4-2 Red Sox victory at Fenway Park.

300
July 9, 2009: A two-run shot off Kansas City's Luke Hochevar in the first inning of an 8-6 loss to the Royals at Fenway Park.

400
July 4, 2012: At Oakland's O.co Coliseum, a solo homer in the fourth inning off A.J. Griffin of the Athletics, who went on to defeat the Red Sox, 3-2.

500
Sept. 12, 2015: At Tropicana Field, the second of two homers Ortiz hit that day off the Rays' Matt Moore, a solo shot in the fifth inning of an eventual 10-4 Red Sox victory.

HOME RUNS
BY TEAM

RED SOX
483

TWINS
58

541

TOTAL CAREER
HOME RUNS

BLASTS, YEAR BY YEAR

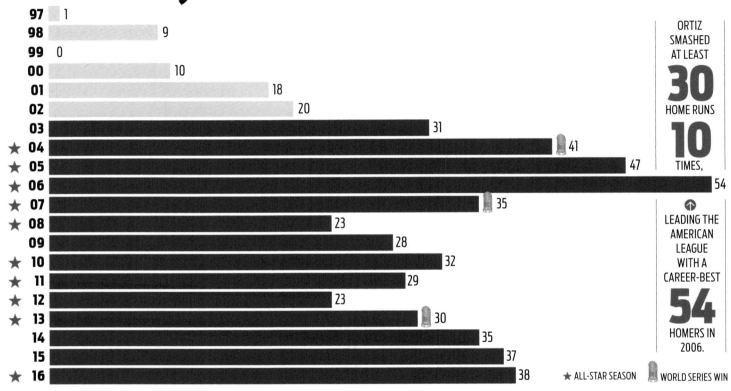

Year	HR
97	1
98	9
99	0
00	10
01	18
02	20
03	31
★ 04	41
★ 05	47
★ 06	54
★ 07	35
★ 08	23
09	28
★ 10	32
★ 11	29
★ 12	23
★ 13	30
14	35
15	37
★ 16	38

ORTIZ SMASHED AT LEAST

30 HOME RUNS

10 TIMES,

⬆

LEADING THE AMERICAN LEAGUE WITH A CAREER-BEST

54 HOMERS IN 2006.

★ ALL-STAR SEASON   🏆 WORLD SERIES WIN

ORTIZ HIT TWO HOME RUNS IN A GAME 51 TIMES, BUT NEVER HIT THREE

6 HOME RUNS

ROY HALLADAY

5 HOME RUNS

JAMIE MOYER

4 HOME RUNS

12 PITCHERS:
Chris Archer, Ramon Ortiz,
Ervin Santana, Joe Blanton,
A.J. Burnett, Josh Towers,
Mark Buehrle, Matt Garza,
Seth McClung, Kevin Millwood,
Gavin Floyd, Gil Meche

HOME RUNS BY COUNT

1-1	76
0-0	74
3-2	69
2-2	60
2-1	54
1-0	52
0-1	45
1-2	37
3-1	30
2-0	29
0-2	9
3-0	6

HOME RUNS BY INNING

1	85
2	37
3	58
4	82
5	73
6	66
7	48
8	48
9	32
Extra	12

HOME RUNS VS. TEAMS

TOR	62
BAL	55
TBR	53
NYY	53
DET	36
TEX	33
LAA	32
SEA	30
CHW	28
CLE	27

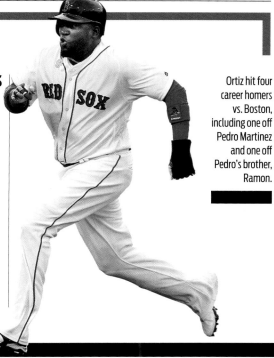

Ortiz hit four career homers vs. Boston, including one off Pedro Martinez and one off Pedro's brother, Ramon.

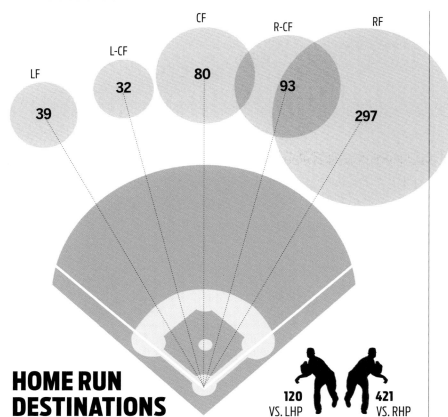

HOME RUN DESTINATIONS

LF **39**
L-CF **32**
CF **80**
R-CF **93**
RF **297**

120 VS. LHP
421 VS. RHP

CAREER MILESTONES

632 DOUBLES (10TH)

541 HOME RUNS (17TH)

1,768 RBIs (22ND)

4,765 TOTAL BASES (31ST)

2,472 HITS (T-103)

Ortiz homered in 29 ballparks off 27 opponents. He had 11 walk-off homers and 11 grand slams.

30 & 100

David Ortiz is the only player in MLB with 30+ HR and 100+ RBI in each of the last four seasons (2013-2016)... **ORTIZ REACHED THOSE TOTALS 10 TIMES** with the Red Sox, most in club history (Ted Williams ranks 2nd with 7). His 10 Boston seasons of 100 RBI also eclipse Williams (9) for most in franchise history.

THE ONLY PLAYERS WITH AT LEAST 10 SEASONS OF 30+ HR AND 100+ RBI FOR A SINGLE TEAM:

Babe Ruth	12, Yankees
Albert Pujols	10, Cardinals
Hank Aaron	10, Braves
Lou Gehrig	10, Yankees
DAVID ORTIZ	**10, RED SOX**

ALL-TIME HOME RUNS (MLB)
15.	Manny Ramirez	555
16.	Mike Schmidt	548
17.	**DAVID ORTIZ**	**541**
18.	Mickey Mantle	536
19.	Jimmie Foxx	534

ALL-TIME HITS (MLB)
101.	Mickey Vernon	2,495
102.	Fred McGriff	2,490
103.	**DAVID ORTIZ**	**2,472**
	Ted Simmons	2,472
105.	Joe Medwick	2,471

ALL-TIME DOUBLES (MLB)
8.	Carl Yastrzemski	646
9.	Honus Wagner	643
10.	**DAVID ORTIZ**	**625**
11.	Hank Aaron	624
12.	Paul Molitor	605
	Paul Waner	605

ALL-TIME DOUBLES (Red Sox)
1.	Carl Yastrzemski	646
2.	Ted Williams	525
3.	**DAVID ORTIZ**	**524**
4.	Dwight Evans	474
5.	Wade Boggs	422

MOST GAMES PLAYED (Red Sox)
1.	Carl Yastrzemski	3,308
2.	Dwight Evans	2,505
3.	Ted Williams	2,292
4.	Jim Rice	2,089
5.	**DAVID ORTIZ**	**1,953**

GAMES AT FENWAY

DAVID ORTIZ APPEARED IN 1,014 REGULAR-SEASON GAMES AT FENWAY PARK (BOS-999, MIN-15)... THE ONLY PLAYERS TO APPEAR IN 1,000 REGULAR-SEASON GAMES AT THE VENUE ARE:

CARL YASTRZEMSKI	**DWIGHT EVANS**	**TED WILLIAMS**	**JIM RICE**	**DAVID ORTIZ**
1,676	1,249	1,165	1,048	1,014

PAPI'S BIG PAYDAYS *ANNUAL SALARY ONLY

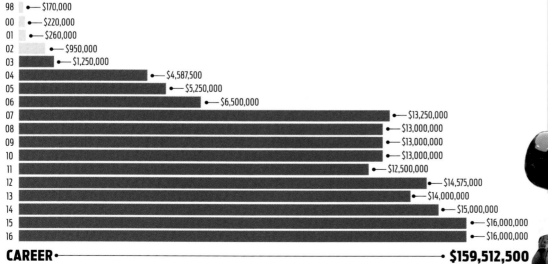

98	$170,000
00	$220,000
01	$260,000
02	$950,000
03	$1,250,000
04	$4,587,500
05	$5,250,000
06	$6,500,000
07	$13,250,000
08	$13,000,000
09	$13,000,000
10	$13,000,000
11	$12,500,000
12	$14,575,000
13	$14,000,000
14	$15,000,000
15	$16,000,000
16	$16,000,000
CAREER	**$159,512,500**

MINNESOTA TWINS   BOSTON RED SOX

SHARED APPRECIATION

OF THE 27 MEMBERS OF THE 500-HOMER CLUB, FIVE HAVE PLAYED FOR THE RED SOX. DAVID ORTIZ HIT NEARLY 90 PERCENT OF HIS CAREER HOMERS WITH BOSTON.

100%

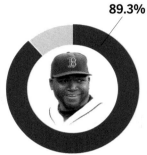

TED WILLIAMS
521 HRs with Red Sox

89.3%

DAVID ORTIZ
483 HRs with Red Sox

49.4%

MANNY RAMIREZ
274 HRs with Red Sox

41.6%

JIMMIE FOXX
222 HRs with Red Sox

6.9%

BABE RUTH
49 HRs with Red Sox

IN 2016, ORTIZ BECAME THE FIRST SOX HITTER WITH

70

OR MORE EXTRA-BASE HITS IN NINE SEASONS, BREAKING A TIE WITH TED WILLIAMS (8 SEASONS).

IN 2016, ORTIZ HELPED THE RED SOX CAPTURE THEIR EIGHTH POSTSEASON BERTH IN 14 SEASONS SINCE HE JOINED THE CLUB IN 2003. IT WAS BOSTON'S 22ND POSTSEASON APPEARANCE ALL-TIME.

REGULAR-SEASON CAREER

Year	Age	Team	Lg	G	AB	R	H	2B	3B	HR	RBI	SB	CS	BB	SO	BA	OBP	SLG	SH	SF	IBB	Pos	Awards
1997	21	MIN	AL	15	49	10	16	3	0	1	6	0	0	2	19	.327	.353	.449	0	0	0	3/D	
1998	22	MIN	AL	86	278	47	77	20	0	9	46	1	0	39	72	.277	.371	.446	0	4	3	3D	
1999	23	MIN	AL	10	20	1	0	0	0	0	0	0	0	5	12	.000	.200	.000	0	0	0	/D3	
2000	24	MIN	AL	130	415	59	117	36	1	10	63	1	0	57	81	.282	.364	.446	0	6	2	D3	
2001	25	MIN	AL	89	303	46	71	17	1	18	48	1	0	40	68	.234	.324	.475	1	2	8	D/3	
2002	26	MIN	AL	125	412	52	112	32	1	20	75	1	2	43	87	.272	.339	.500	0	8	0	D3	
2003	27	BOS	AL	128	448	79	129	39	2	31	101	0	0	58	83	.288	.369	.592	0	2	8	D3	MVP-5
2004	28	BOS	AL	150	582	94	175	47	3	41	139	0	0	75	133	.301	.380	.603	0	8	8	★D3	AS,MVP-4,SS
2005	29	BOS	AL	159	601	119	180	40	1	47	148	1	0	102	124	.300	.397	.604	0	9	9	★D3	AS,MVP-2,SS
2006	30	BOS	AL	151	558	115	160	29	2	54	137	1	0	119	117	.287	.413	.636	0	5	23	★D3	AS,MVP-3,SS
2007	31	BOS	AL	149	549	116	182	52	1	35	117	3	1	111	103	.332	.445	.621	0	3	12	★D/3	AS,MVP-4,SS
2008	32	BOS	AL	109	416	74	110	30	1	23	89	1	0	70	74	.264	.369	.507	1	3	12	★D	AS
2009	33	BOS	AL	150	541	77	129	35	1	28	99	0	2	74	134	.238	.332	.462	0	7	5	★D/3	
2010	34	BOS	AL	145	518	86	140	36	1	32	102	0	1	82	145	.270	.370	.529	0	4	14	★D/3	AS
2011	35	BOS	AL	146	525	84	162	40	1	29	96	1	1	78	83	.309	.398	.554	0	1	12	★D/3	AS,SS
2012	36	BOS	AL	90	324	65	103	26	0	23	60	0	1	56	51	.318	.415	.611	0	3	13	D/3	AS
2013	37	BOS	AL	137	518	84	160	38	2	30	103	4	0	76	88	.309	.395	.564	0	5	27	★D/3	AS,MVP-10,SS
2014	38	BOS	AL	142	518	59	136	27	0	35	104	0	0	75	95	.263	.355	.517	0	6	22	★D/3	
2015	39	BOS	AL	146	528	73	144	37	0	37	108	0	1	77	95	.273	.360	.553	0	9	16	★D/3	MVP-28
2016	40	BOS	AL	151	537	79	169	48	1	38	127	2	0	80	86	.315	401	.620	0	7	15	★D/3	AS
20 Years				2408	8640	1419	2472	632	19	541	1768	17	9	1319	1750	.286	.380	.552	2	92	209		
162 Game Average				162	581	96	167	43	1	36	119	1	1	89	118	.286	.380	.552	0	6	14		
BOS (14 yrs)				1953	7163	1204	2079	524	16	483	1530	13	7	1133	1411	.290	.386	.570	1	72	196		
MIN (6 yrs)				455	1477	215	393	108	3	58	238	4	2	186	339	.266	.348	.461	1	20	13		

★ INDICATES HE MADE THE AMERICAN LEAGUE ALL-STAR TEAM THAT SEASON, SS=SILVER SLUGGER; MVP-# INDICATES FINISH IN MVP BALLOTING

POSTSEASON CAREER

	G	AB	R	H	2B	3B	HR	RBI	SB	CS	BB	SO	BA	OBP	SLG	OPS
9 Yrs (18 Series)	85	304	51	88	22	2	17	61	0	1	59	72	.289	.404	.543	.947
9 ALDS	32	115	16	31	10	0	6	17	0	0	23	29	.270	.388	.513	.902
6 ALCS	39	145	21	37	6	2	8	30	0	1	22	38	.255	.357	.490	.846
3 World Series	14	44	14	20	6	0	3	14	0	0	14	5	.455	.576	.795	1.372

CREDITS AND ACKNOWLEDGMENTS

BOSTON GLOBE PHOTOGRAPHS AND ILLUSTRATIONS BY

Peter Abraham, 130-132; Keith Bedford, 101, 110, 116; John Bohn, 39; Yoon S. Byun, 126; Barry Chin, 28, 31, 34-35, 38-39, 46-47, 84, 102, 106-107, 110, 128, back cover; Tonia Cowan, 94; Jim Davis, 4, 6, 7, 13, 23-27, 29-33, 36, 40-41, 43, 46-47, 50, 52-53, 55, 60, 66, 71, 79, 84-88, 96, 100, 101-102, 104, 107-108, 110, 113, 125, 129, 138, 140, 143-144; Bill Greene, 40, 43, 46; Pat Greenhouse, 18, 78; Stan Grossfeld, 2, 10, 14, 22, 43-44, 56, 73-75, 92, 126-127, 143; Matthew J. Lee, 21, 25, 26, 34, 83; Jessica Rinaldi, 77, 90, 137; David L. Ryan, 134; John Tlumacki, front cover, 31, 40, 42, 45, 69, 80, 84, 86, 91, 93, 99, 102, 107, 110, 115, 123, 139, 141; Craig F. Walker, 119-120; Jonathan Wiggs, 61, 122.

ADDITIONAL PHOTOGRAPHS COURTESY OF

AP/Wide World Photos, 93 (Elise Amendola); Boston Red Sox, 8 (Julie Cordeiro), 9 (Brita Meng Outzen); Getty Images, 1 (Ronald Martinez), 41 (Stephen Dunn), 42 (Al Bello), 60 (Ezra Shaw), 70 (Jared Wickerham), 103 (Jim McIsaac); Reuters, 63 (Eduardo Munoz).

WITH SPECIAL THANKS TO

Boston Globe publisher John W. Henry, chief executive officer Mike Sheehan, and editor Brian McGrory; Joe Sullivan and the Globe sports department; Gordon Edes; Bill Greene and the Globe photo department; Lisa Tuite and the Globe library staff; Mitch Rogatz, Kristine Anstrats, Patricia Frey, and everyone at Triumph Books; Zachary Shuster Harmsworth Literary Agency.